The Incomparableness of God

In His Being, Attributes, Works, and Word

by George Swinnock

*For who in the heavens can be compared
to the Lord?
Who among the sons of the mighty can be
likened to the Lord?*

Psalm 89:6

Contents

ANALYTICAL OUTLINE

SECTION ONE: EXPOSITION
I. God is incomparable in his being
    [God in comparison to false gods]
        i. In comparison to demons
        ii. In comparison to idols
    1. God is from himself
    2. God is being
    3. God is an independent being
    5. God is a universal being
    6. God is an unchangeable being
    7. God is an eternal being
        (1). God has no beginning
        (2). God has no succession
        (3). God hath no ending
    8. God is a simple being
    9. God is an infinite being
    10. God is an incomprehensible being
II. God is incomparable in his attributes
    1. Generally
        (1). In his holiness
        (2). In his wisdom
        (3). In his power
        (4). In his justice
        (5). In his knowledge
            i. The object of his knowledge
            ii. The manner of his knowledge
        (6). In his truth and faithfulness
            i. In his works
            ii. In his words
        (7). In his mercy
        (8). In his patience
            i. How perfectly he hateth sin
            ii. What an affront sin is to him
            iii. Who dares and provokes him

        iv. He knoweth all men's sins

        v. He is able to avenge himself

        vi. He is more provoked because of his patience

        vii. He bears with sin many years

        viii. He does good to sinners

  2. More specifically.

      (1). These attributes are essential to God

      (2). These attributes are the essence of God

      (3). These attributes are all one in God

      (4). These attributes are in God infinitely

III. God is incomparable in his works

  1. His works themselves

      (1). Creation

      (2). Providence

        i. For preservation

        ii. For gubernation

      (3). The work of redemption

  2. He is incomparable in what he can do

  3. The manner of his working

      (1). He works irresistibly

      (2). He work arbitrarily

      (3). He works at without weariness

      (4). He work wholly by his own power

IV. God is incomparable in his word

  1. He is incomparable in the manner of his word

      (1). He speaks authoritatively

      (2). He speaks condescendingly

      (3). He speaks effectually

  2. God is incomparable in the matter of his word

      (1). The purity of its precepts

      (2). The mystery of its doctrines

      (3). The prophecies and predictions of the word

  3. God is incomparable in the effects of his word

      (1). In converting the soul

      (2). In affrighting the sinner

      (3). In healing the wounded spirit

SECTION TWO: APPLICATION

I. By way of information

1. Of the great venom and malignity of sin
    (1). Sin is a breach of this God's law
    (2). Sin is a contempt of God's authority
    (3). Sin is a dishonouring of God
    (4). Sin is a fighting with God
2. Of the madness and misery of sinners
    (1). Their madness
        i. In daring to offend him
        ii. In those who will venture the eternal loss of his God
    (2). Their misery
        i. They must depart forever from this incomparable God.
        ii. They shall have this incomparable God for their enemy
3. Of the pride and presumption of those who compare themselves with God
    (1). When they quarrel with the precepts of God
    (2). When they question the providences of God
    (3). When they tax the decrees of God
    (4). When those in authority usurp God's authority
4. Of the incomparable service and worship due to him
    (1). God calls for incomparable awe and reverence.
    (2). God calls for incomparable humility and lowliness of spirit
    (3). God calls for incomparable love, the top, the cream of our affections
    (4). God must have incomparable trust
    (5). God must have incomparable obedience in the whole course of our lives
5. Of his infinite grace and condescension
II. By way of counsel
    1. Study the knowledge of this God
        (1). It is a sanctifying knowledge.
        (2). It is a satisfying knowledge.
        (3). It is a saving knowledge.
        The means which to attain knowledge:
            i. Be sensible of ignorance
            ii. Study the works word of God
            iii. Pray that God would give you the knowledge of himself
    2. Choose God for your portion and happiness
        (1). Consider what is offered you in God

(2). Consider how you may have this God

(3). Consider for what end God offers himself to you

That you may give God the praise of incomparable perfections. Consider—

      i. God is excellency itself

      ii. God is the standard of excellency

      iii. God is so excellent that even angels veil their faces in his presence

      iv. God is so excellent that he humbles himself to take notice of his angels

      v. God is so excellent that he is above the highest worship of his creatures

      vi. God is so excellent that his excellencies are beyond the understanding of creatures

III. By way of comfort

    1. This incomparable God is yours

    2. All the incomparable excellencies of this God are yours

    3. This incomparable God will be thine forever

EDITOR'S INTRODUCTION

I only have a few small notes to give to the reader before he embarks on the wonderful journey of reading this text. Swinnock has structured this text into two large sections, the exposition of God's incomparableness (chapters 1-17) and the application of God's incomparableness (chapters 18-26). Within each section, I have attempted to standardize the numbering system he uses for his various lists because they are often extensive and span chapters. I have used the following numbering system in both sections (though I have not indented the items in the text):

I.
   1.
      (1).
         i.

Occasionally, as in chapters 13 and 15, there is a list introduced which is neither a continuation of the immediately prior list nor nested under the last item in it, nor of a part with the following list, but is still related to the same overall topic. In these cases, I have used the lower case roman numerals because these sections do not come in the context of other lists on that level, though it should be noted that it is not conceptually subordinate to that last item of the previous list. I have also left any numbering within a paragraph unchanged.

Any text in brackets is added by me to clarify Swinnock's meaning. All footnotes are mine. Any untranslated Latin and Greek I have translated in the footnotes, though Swinnock translates much of the Latin himself. Occasionally, Swinnock's translation is more of a paraphrase and in those cases I have added a more literal translation in the footnotes.

I would like to thank Jonah Litwiller and Trent Alderfer for reading through the first edition and bearing with the typos as well as offering their edifying thoughts on the content. This second edition is better as a result.

Soli Deo Gloria,
T. G. Drummond
Harleysville
March, 2020

THE EPISTLE DEDICATORY

To the Worshipful HENRY ASHURST, Junior, Esq.; and to the Honourable Lady DIANA ASHURST, his Religious Consort.

SUCH is the excellency of the soul of man, that the very heathen, whose
souls were almost wholly immersed in grease and sensuality, and served
but as salt to preserve their bodies for a time from putrefaction, according
to the opinion of one of the most ingenious among them, have acknowl-
edged it a divine plant, a drop of the ocean of being, a ray of a deity; and
the body but the case or cabinet of this jewel. The dim rushlight of nature
hath enabled some of them to discern the spirituality, quick, comprehensive, self-reflective motions, and immortality of their specific forms, as
they called their souls, and thence to conclude their worth and nobleness.
But the clear sunlight of Scripture advantageth unto a fuller discovery of
its excellency. It shows us its original, that it is of celestial extraction, created immediately by the Father of spirits, a beam of the Sun of righteousness, a bubble of the fountain of life, of a much higher descent than the
house of clay and earthly tabernacle, the body, Gen. 2:7; Heb. 12:9; Zech.
12:1. It acquaints us with its duration, that it runs parallel with the line of
eternity, and swallows up years, and ages, and generations, and thousands
of thousands, and millions of millions, as small drops and minutes and
nothings, in the bottomless ocean and endlessness of its abode and continuance. When the body, like the sacrifice, falleth to the earth and is turned
into ashes, the soul, like the flame, aspireth and ascendeth to God, Eccles.
12:7; Phil. 1:23; Mat. 10:28, 22:31, 32. It manifesteth the soul's capacity, how
no being is excepted from its consideration, all are within its compass and
horizon; it can view every [being] with its intellectual eye. It is not bounded
with corporeal beings, nor limited with material objects, nor circumscribed
with created essences, but is capable of apprehending the first cause, the
being of beings, the original of all things. It is able not only to retrospect

upon its own motions, and to survey the several parts, and ranks, and orders, and rarities, and delicacies, and excellencies of the earth and this sublunary world, but also to ascend to the highest heavens, and behold the beautiful face of the blessed God, till it hath looked itself into the very likeness, and thereby rendered itself fit and meet for his dearest love and eternal embraces.

The excellency of our souls doth eminently appear in its receptiveness of the divine image. Great princes do not stamp their image on mean things, as brass and pewter, but on the most excellent metals, as silver and gold, Eph. 4:23, 24; Col. 3:10; Gen. 1:26. And its capableness of enjoying immediately the blessed God. To stand before kings doth both speak and make a person honourable and worthy, Prov. 22:29. God alone is the fountain of honour and the standard of excellency, Isa. 43:5. Every being is his coin, and he stampeth on it the rate it shall go at. The holiness and happiness of the rational creature consisteth in these two: his holiness, in conformity to God; his happiness, in communion with him. And these two have a dependence on each other. They only who are like him, can enjoy him. 'If we say we have fellowship with him, and walk in darkness, we lie, and the truth is not in us,' 1 John 1:6. Holiness, or the image of God, is not only an indispensable condition, without which no man shall enjoy God, Heb. 12:14; John 3:3; but withal an absolutely necessary disposition, without which no man can enjoy God, Col. 1:12; 2 Cor. 5. And as conformity disposeth for communion, so communion increaseth conformity; vision causeth assimilation in nature, Gen. 31:38, 39; grace, 2 Cor. 3:18; and glory, 1 John 3:2.

Though the motions of the understanding and will are in some respect circular, yet the understanding is the first mover and the leading faculty, and so the knowledge of the blessed God is both antecedent to, and productive of, this image. Though the knowledge of creatures puffeth up, polluteth, and so debaseth and destroyeth the soul, sinking it the deeper into hell, as a vessel laden with silver and gold and the most precious commodities, when it miscarrieth, sinketh the deeper for its weight and burden, 1 Cor. 8:1; Luke 12:47, 48; yet the knowledge of God is humbling, advancing, purifying, and saving, Job 42; 2 Pet. 3:18; John 17:3. The incomparable excellency of the boundless blessed God is the subject of this treatise, which I present to you both as a testimony of the honour and service I owe to you, and of my desire to be instrumental for your spiritual and eternal good. The subject is the highest imaginable; and though the manner of handling it be plain and ordinary, and infinitely below and unbecoming the divine majesty—'For who can express his noble acts, or display all his praise,' Ps. 106:2—yet the matter of it doth deserve, and may prevail for your acceptance of it.

If knowledge be the excellency of a man, and differenceth him from a beast, surely then divine knowledge, or the knowledge of God in Christ, is the excellency of a Christian, and differenceth him from other men. Our awe of, love to, and trust in the divine Majesty, are founded in the right knowledge of him. Creatures, the more they are known, the less they are esteemed; but the more the blessed God is known, the more he is prized, desired, and obeyed, Ps. 73:25; 76:7; 90:11; 9:10. Our hatred of sin and contempt of the world proceed from our acquaintance with God. He only hath hateful thoughts of sin, and self-loathing apprehensions because of it, who hath seen the great and glorious, the good and gracious God, whose authority is contemned, whose law is violated, whose name is dishonoured, whose image is defaced, and whose love is abused by it, Job 42:6; Isa. 6:5. He only lives above this present evil world, and all the riches and honours and pleasures thereof, who can look beyond it to the infinite God, and those unsearchable riches and weights of glory, and rivers of pleasures that are in and with him. That which was rich and glorious and pleasant to a soul before, hath now no worth, no glory, no pleasure, by reason of that wealth and glory and pleasure which doth so infinitely exceed. When the God of glory appeared to Abraham, he quickly and quietly left his country and kindred, and followed God, not knowing whither he went, Gen. 12:1, 2; Acts 7:3. If the God of glory appear to your souls, you will soon wink upon these withering vanities, broken cisterns, and gilded nothings, and count them all but dung and dross, for the excellency of the knowledge of him in Christ.

You have begun well, go on and persevere in well-doing. I shall give you the same counsel which the holy apostle giveth to those of whom he was persuaded that they had those things which accompanied salvation, Heb. 6:9. 'Take heed lest there be in you an evil heart of unbelief, whereby ye should depart away from the living God,' Heb. 3:12. 'Look diligently, lest ye should fail of the grace of God,' Heb. 12:15. When false coin is common abroad, we are the more careful what money we take; when much false grace is up and down amongst us, and so many please themselves with their profession, or spiritual privileges, or sacred performances, or siding with this or that party, and form of worship, or the respect and repute they have with others; it concerns you to be the more suspicious of yourselves, lest you should fail of that grace of God which conformeth the heart to the nature, and the life to the will and law of God.

SIR,—You are descended of a worthy, ancient, and religious family; your grandfather, as I have heard, was eminent for holiness; your father is noted and honoured for one that feareth God above many; you have hereby the more encouragement, advantage, and engagement to exercise yourself to godliness. Tamerlane made it his practice to read often the heroic deeds of his progenitors, not as proud of them, or boasting in them, but as glorious patterns, to inflame his soul with a love of their virtues. Man is a creature that is led more by the eye than the ear, by patterns than by precepts; and no patterns are more prevalent than of those whom nature and grace oblige us to esteem and affect. These examples, above all others, as flaming beacons on a hill, call us to a stout defence of virtue, when it is invaded by its enemies. Alexander, finding one of his name cowardly, charged him to change his name, or to become valiant. When one of the Scipios, descended of Scipio Africanus, became dissolute, the Roman senate ordered him to put off that ring which he wore as the badge of his noble family, because, by his vicious life, he was a reproach to it. The truth is, a wicked son of a godly father, as Uriah, carrieth letters of his own condemnation about him, causing the patterns and precepts of his family to be auxiliaries to his own reproach and infamy; whilst the light and lustre of his ancestors renders his works of darkness the more gross and palpable. I mention not these things as suspecting your integrity, but to provoke and quicken you to the greater care and circumspection in your carriage and conversation.

MADAM,—Your birth is honourable, but such honour without holiness extends not beyond the meridian of this world; grace only is eternal glory. That honour which is woven in the finest tapestry of earthly privileges will lose colour, and fade away; but the knowledge of God is a possession forever. Nobility by parents is but nobility by parchment, and that is but skin-deep at most, and will waste with time. Godliness alone is that nobility which no age can consume, and which will run parallel with the line of eternity.

The whole earth hath not a pleasanter sight than greatness joined with goodness. Greatness itself is venerable, but goodness joined with it, addeth a new splendour and lustre to it; as a sparkling diamond set in a gold ring, it attracteth the eyes, and challengeth a greater reverence and respect from all. Evil greatness is a swelling dropsy, a disease of the body politic, as intolerable a burden as the earth groans under; but grace and virtue are the more excellent and amiable by the greatness of the person in whom they dwell. It will be your crown and credit to prefer God before the world, to esteem holiness as the only beauty, and a title to the covenant as the only riches of your immortal soul.

Ye have both near and dear relations, whose hearts will rejoice in your perseverance and progress in the ways of God's commandments; that you may be helps to each other in the best things, provoke one another to love, and to good works, live long together on earth, and forever together in heaven, is the prayer

Of your servant in the Lord,

GEORGE SWINNOCK

I

EXPOSITION OF GOD'S INCOMPARABLENESS

I

THE PREFACE AND MEANING OF THE TEXT

It is certain, that our happiness in the other world will consist in part in our perfect knowledge of the blessed and boundless God: when we shall 'know him as we are known of him,' we shall be blessed as he is blessed; and when 'we shall see him as he is, we shall be like him' in purity and felicity; we shall be fully satisfied with his likeness and his love. Rich must be the delight which the most large and noble faculty of man, his understanding, shall receive, in its intimate acquaintance with, and clear and full apprehension of, the highest truth. And it is as certain, that our holiness in this world doth not a little depend upon our knowledge of him, whose 'name alone is excellent.' None wander from him, prefer the flesh and world before him, and in their whole lives walk contrary to him, but from their ignorance of him. 'They are estranged from the life of God, (i.e., a spiritual heavenly conversation,) through the ignorance that is in them, because of the blindness of their hearts,' Eph. 4:18. Dark corners of a house are filled with dust, dark cellars with vermin, and dark hearts with cursed lusts: none are enlarged in desires after God, or ravished with delight in God, or can cast their souls and all their concerns on God, but those that are acquainted with him. They who know his beauty and bounty, cannot but love him, and they who know his power and faithfulness, cannot but trust him; 'They who know thy name will put their trust in thee,' Ps. 9:10. Whence comes it to pass, that believers can trample on the riches and treasures, and wealth of this beggarly world, that they can lay their white and yellow earth, their silver and gold, at the apostles' feet, that they can suffer the spoiling of their goods, not only patiently, but joyfully, Heb. 10:34, but from the knowledge of him who is true riches, Luke 16:11; substance, Prov. 8:21; an enduring substance, Job 10:3–4; a bottomless mine of unsearchable riches, Eph. 3:8? Whence is it, that they can refuse to be called the sons of king's daughters, that they can contemn honours and preferments, spurn crowns and sceptres under their feet, but from the knowledge of him who is their crown of glory, their diadem of renown, and the praise of all his saints, Heb.

11:24, 25? That which to the sensual worldling is so glorious, hath no glory in the believer's eye, by reason of the Lord of glory, who doth so infinitely excel. Whence is it, that they can hate father, mother, wife, child, liberty, yea, life itself, and leave all at the call and command of their Maker, but from the knowledge of him who is, as Elkanah said to Hannah, better to them than ten sons, than all relations, than the whole creation? Those stars vanish and disappear, when once the Sun of righteousness ariseth: how quickly, how quietly, without any hesitancy or reluctancy, will Abraham leave his country, and kindred, and father's house, when once 'the God of glory appeareth to him,' Acts 9:2-4. In a word, whence is it that 'they escape the pollutions of the world,' in which others are mired, drowned, and destroyed, 'but through the knowledge of God,' 2 Pet. 2:20? Well may our Lord Jesus say, 'It is life eternal, to know thee the only true God, and Jesus Christ whom thou hast sent.' To know God affectionately, as our chiefest good, so as to give him our superlative esteem, and intensest love, is spiritual life here, in the habit or principle, as also in the act and exercise of it; and it is the beginning, seed, preparation, and way of our eternal life hereafter. But who can know that being which infinitely passeth all knowledge? He that would know God fully, must be God himself; and he who would tell you what God is, in any measure answerable to his excellency, had need 'to know him as he is known of him.' And supposing I were able to speak of the perfection of God, as one that, like the great apostle, had been caught up 'into the third heavens:' I question whether, if I had a tongue to speak of him after that manner, ye had ears to hear of him, or hearts to understand what I should speak. But though I am not able to speak, nor you to hear of God, according to his perfection, yet through the assistance of the Holy Ghost so much may be spoken and heard of him, as may tend to our present sanctification and future salvation. Though we cannot 'see him as he is,' yet we may see him as he is not; though the height of his being be above the reach of our understandings, we may get somewhat nearer to him, and indeed we have no other way while we are here, than by climbing upon the shoulders of all created excellencies, and there proclaiming, 'That none in the heavens is to be compared to the Lord, that none among the sons of the mighty is like unto the Lord." [Ps. 98:6].

In the words, the Psalmist compareth God with, and preferreth God before, the highest, the greatest in heaven and earth.

In the words we have a comparison and a prelation.

i. A comparison, and this is between God and those that are most excellent in heaven, and the mightiest on earth.

ii. A prelation, or preferring God before whatsoever is excellent in heaven or earth: the interrogation is a strong negation, as is frequent in Scripture, Prov. 20:9; 'Who can say I have made my heart clean, I am pure from my sin?' i.e., none can say I have made my heart clean, or am pure from my sin; so Exod. 15:11, 'Who is like to thee, O Lord, among the gods? Who is like thee, glorious in holiness, fearful in praises, doing wonders?' that is, none is like thee among the gods, none is so glorious in holiness, so fearful in praises, such a wonder-working God as thou art. Thus the Psalmist understandeth the text; 'For who in the heavens is to be compared to the Lord? Who among the sons of the mighty can be likened to the Lord?' i.e., none in the heavens, none among the sons of the mighty on earth is comparable to Jehovah.

I shall first give you the meaning of the words, and then lay down the doctrine, which will be the foundation of my discourse on the subject.

For; this causal particle gives the reason why saints and angels should join together in the praise of God. 'The heavens shall praise thy wonders, O Lord, thy faithfulness also in the congregation of the saints: for who in the heavens is to be compared to the Lord?' ver. 5. By the heavens, Calvin understandeth the holy angels, who rejoice in the church's welfare, and bless God for preserving his people, and performing his promises to them; and it is apparent by the apostle, that angels are present in the congregation of the saints, 1 Cor. 11:11. And so this text addeth another ground for their admiration of the great God; viz., his incomparable excellency. His high and matchless perfections call for high and matchless praises. Others take the text as a ground for the confirmation of the Psalmist's faith in the covenant God had made with him, mentioned verse 3, 4, namely, God's superiority over angels in heaven, and men on earth; therefore they cannot hinder him in the accomplishment of his word, being infinitely inferior to him.

Who in the heavens? Who in the sky? Ainsworth reads it. In the clouds, *in nubibus, æquabitur*, is to be equalled, saith Calvin, to Jehovah, *Quis enim in superiore nube par æstimetur Jehova.* Who in the higher clouds is equal to Jehovah, so Tremell reads it.

Who in the heavens? I.e., say some, in the starry heavens, among the celestial bodies, sun, moon, or stars; which were adored as gods, not only by the Persians, but also by some idolatrous Jews, because of their brightness and beauty, their lustre and glory. Which of all those famous lamps, and heavenly luminaries, is to be compared to the Father of lights, and Sun of righteousness? They may glister like glowworms in the night of paganism, among them who are covered with the mantle of darkness, but when this Sun ariseth, and day appeareth, they all vanish and disappear.

Who in the heavens? I.e., say others, in the heaven of heavens, the highest, the third heavens, among the celestial spirits, cherubims and seraphims, angels and archangels, principalities and powers, thrones and dominions? Who among the innumerable company of angels? Who among those pure, those perfect spirits, who are the ancientest, the honourablest house of the creation, is to be compared to the Father of spirits?

Though angels are glorious creatures, considered simply, and in themselves, in respect of their power, wisdom, purity, and beauty; yet if they be considered comparatively with the blessed God, I may say of them as the apostle doth of the Jewish worship, which was glorious, by reason of its divine institution, in comparison with the Christian worship: 2 Cor. 3:10, 'Even that which was glorious, had no glory in this respect, by reason of the glory that excelleth.'

Is to be compared to Jehovah? Is to be likened to Jehovah? Is to be equalled to Jehovah? Is to be put in the scales, and worthy to be weighed with Jehovah, that being of beings, that God of gods.

To Jehovah? This name Jehovah is the chief and most proper name of God. It is derived from *haiah, fuit*[1], and signifieth that being which was, is, and is to come; which is always the same, and the cause of all other beings, Rev. 1:4, 6; Ps. 102:28; Acts 17:28, and which gives a being to his word and promises. In heaven there is among glorious angels no such being.

Who amongst the sons of the mighty? *Inter filios fortium.*[2] Who among the sons of the strong, Jun.[3] reads it. Among the sons of the gods, saith Calvin; so the Seventy read it,[4] and understand, with the Chaldee paraphrase, angels, who are called sons of God, Job 1:6, and 38:7. But we, having understood angels, the best and highest in heaven, by the first interrogation, 'Who in the heavens is to be compared to the Lord?' it may be most convenient to understand in this place, by sons of the mighty, the best and

---

[1] *Haiah* is a transliteration of the Hebrew copula, היה, "he is." *Fuit* is the perfect third person singular of the Latin copula, *est*, "he is."
[2] "Among the sons of the mighty."
[3] Franciscus Junius (1545-1602), in his Biblia, Psalm 89:7.
[4] "The Seventy" refers to the Septuagint (LXX), the Greek translation of the Old Testament, which, according to Jewish tradition, was made by seventy scribes who, all working independently, created the exact same translation. The LXX reads, ἐν υἱοῖς θεοῦ, "among the sons of God."

highest on earth, the greatest and most gracious princes and potentates, who are higher by head and shoulders than others. These are called gods, and sons of the Most High, or Almighty, Ps. 82:6. And hereby the prophet challengeth both worlds, heaven and earth, to bring forth any that may equal or compare with Jehovah.

Can be likened to the Lord? Is such a being as he is, can speak, or act as he doth; is in any respect worthy to be named with him.

II

GOD IS INCOMPARABLE IN HIS BEING

The doctrine which I shall raise out of the words is this, That God is incomparable; or, there is none among the highest, the holiest, in heaven or earth, like unto Jehovah. Take the greatest, the most excellent of beings in this or the other world, yet they come infinitely short of this being of beings: Ps. 86:8, 'Among the gods there is none like unto thee, O Lord.' Mark, the psalmist doth not choose a weak adversary for God to contend with and conquer, but the strongest. He doth not compare God with the meanest and lowest, but even with the highest, and prefers God before them. 'Among the gods there is none like unto thee, O Lord.'

i. Among those that are gods by unjust usurpation, as evil angels are, who are called the princes of the powers of the air, Eph. 2:2; and the gods of this world, 2 Cor. 4:4. Or, as antichrist, who 'exalteth himself above all that is called God, or is worshipped; so that he as god sitteth in the temple of God, shewing himself that he is God,' 2 Thes. 2:4. Among these, there is none like unto thee, O Lord. These unclean beasts are unworthy to be mentioned with the high, the holy God.

ii. Among those that are gods by men's erroneous persuasions and opinions, as idols, and those deities which the heathen worship, there is none like to thee, o Lord. 'Their idols are silver and gold, the work of men's hands: They have mouths, but they speak not, eyes have they, but they see not. They have ears, but they hear not; noses have they, but they smell not: They have hands, but they handle not; feet have they, but they walk not, neither speak they through their throats,' Ps. 115:4–7. Idols are the work of the creatures, and their makers are infinitely below the Creator; therefore they themselves are much more. 'We know that an idol is nothing in the world, and that there is none other God but one,' 1 Cor. 8:4. Though an idol be somewhat materially, yet it is nothing formally, as to the intent or purpose for which it is worshipped.

1. Among those that are gods by divine ordination, as angels, Ps. 8:5; magistrates, Ps. 82:6, who have the image of a deity stamped on them, in their authority and dominion over others, none is to be compared to Jehovah. These are gods by derivation, by deputation; as subordinate magistrates are commissionated by the supreme, and have a beam of his power communicated to them, but still remain weak creatures, limited by his precepts, and liable to his judgment. So angels and kings have some impressions of a deity on them, but their power is derivative from God, and limited by his will; yea, their essence is from him, their subsistence is by him, and their dependence is every moment upon him. Hence he is called the Most High: Ps. 92:1, 'O thou Most High.' Kings and princes are high, angels and archangels are higher; but Jehovah only is the Most High; Eccles. 5:8, 'He that is higher than the highest considereth.'

For the explication of this doctrine, the truth of it will be evident, if we consider the true God, and compare him with the highest and most excellent in heaven and earth.

    I.   In his being.
    II. In his attributes.
   III. In his works.
   IV. In his word.

I. God is incomparable in his being; God hath not only a being, but an excellency in his being; therefore he is called his excellency: 'Should not his excellency make you afraid,' Job 13:11. And he is said alone to be excellent: 'Thy name alone is excellent,' Ps. 148:13.

By name is meant sometimes anything whereby God makes himself known, Exod. 20:7. But here the being of God, or God himself, as Prov. 18:10, 'The name of the Lord is a strong tower'; i.e., God himself is a strong tower: Ps. 76:1, 'His name is great in Israel;'i.e., the being of the great God is magnified in his church, or among his chosen. Now his being alone is excellent, because there is no such being as his; there is no being excellent besides his, because there is no being excellent like his. He is excellent in all, above all, and beyond all.

His being is such a being, that he alone is, and all besides are nonentities, and no beings in comparison of him. His name speaks the incomparable nature of his being. 'And God said unto Moses, Thus shalt thou say unto the children of Israel, I Am hath sent thee.' I Am, I, a being that really is, beside whom there is none, hath sent thee. What prince, what potentate can say I Am? What angel, what archangel can say I Am? No, this is the proper name of Jehovah.

Therefore, when he promiseth himself to be the reward of his people, he doth promise himself under the notion of essence, being, substance, in opposition to all others, which are but shadows and nothings to him. Prov. 2:7, 'He layeth up sound wisdom (Heb., *essentiam*, essence) for the righteous.' Prov. 8:21, 'I will cause them that love me to inherit substance.' Junius reads it, *Ut possideant id quod est*[5]—I will cause them that love me to possess that which is. God is, and all other beings are not, in comparison of him; Dan. 4:35, 'All the inhabitants of the earth are reputed as nothing.' God is, and all others are nothing; yea, if it were possible to apprehend it, less than nothing. It is a notable expression of the Holy Ghost, to set forth the excellency of God's being; and the pitifulness, meanness, and nothingness of all other beings, Isa. 40:15–17. Behold! (a note of attention and admiration) the nations (the Chaldeans, that are our lords and masters, or all nations of the world, be they never so high, great, strong, or glorious) are as the drop of a bucket (which falleth from the bucket, or hangeth on it, when the water is poured out, yet diminisheth not the measure,) and the small dust of the balance, (which cleaveth to the scales when the spice is put out, yet altereth not the weight, it is so little.) Behold! (wonder, be amazed at it,) he taketh up the isles, (the great, large, vast islands of the world,) as a very little thing, (as poor, small, inconsiderable things.) All nations before him are as nothing. Not only the great islands, but also the continents, with the several innumerable creatures in them, are not only little to this God, but as nothing, as no being to his being, and they are counted to him less than nothing and vanity. Put them in the scales with God, and they are not only light, and without any weight, nothing at all; but if men were capable of conceiving anything less than nothing, such were all the world to God. Though the world be absolutely somewhat, yea, very great, yet comparatively to God it is nothing, less than nothing and vanity.

---

[5] "In order that they might possess that which is."

III

THE INCOMPARABLENESS OF GOD IN HIS BEING. IT IS FROM ITSELF, FOR ITSELF, AND WHOLLY INDEPENDENT

The incomparableness of the divine being will appear in several particulars.

1. His being is from himself. No being in the world, beside his, is its own cause or original. Angels, men, the highest, yea, the lowest creatures, are derivative beings. They have what they are from another, even from God. They are drops that flow from the ocean of all beings; they are rays derived from the sun, the fountain of light and entity. The apostle tells us that men are beholden to God for their beings, Acts 17:28. In him we have our beings. They were nothing till he spake them into something. He formed and fashioned their bodies, Ps. 139:13–15. He created and infused their souls; he put that heaven-born inhabitant into the house of clay, Gen. 2:7; Job 10:11, 12. The whole visible world is his workmanship, Acts 17:24. God that made the world, and all things therein; the invisible world are also the effects of his powerful word. Angels, as well as men, may thank him for what they are. The greatest angel is as much bound to him for his being as the smallest atom; Col. 1:16, 'For by him were all things created that are in heaven and that are in earth, visible and invisible, whether they be thrones or dominions, or principalities or powers.' But God is beholden to none for his being; he was when none else was, even from eternity, Ps. 90:1. Therefore none could contribute the least to his being. I am Jehovah, and there is none else besides me, Isa. 45:5, 6. I am he that giveth a being to himself, that am what I am from myself and of myself, and there is no such being beside me.

2. God is being, that is, for himself; as he is his own first cause, so he is his own last end; as he is wholly from himself, so he is wholly for himself. All other beings are not for themselves, but for another. 'All things were created by him and for him,' Col. 1:16. Since all are from God, it is but reason

that all should be for God. The rivers that run from the sea return to the
sea again, owning and acknowledging their original, Eccles. 1:7. Good men
are for God. 'None of us liveth to himself, or dieth to himself; but whether
we live, we live unto the Lord; and whether we die, we die unto the Lord;
and whether we live or die, we are the Lord's,' Rom. 14:7. Good angels are
for God, for his glory, Isa. 6:3. Evil men, evil angels are for God, though not
in their intentions and purposes, yet in his intention, and by his wise, powerful government of them and their practices; Prov. 16:4, 'The Lord made
all things for himself, even the wicked for the day of slaughter.' Good beings are for him intentionally, and evil beings are for him eventually. Nay,
all beings are for him; of him, and through him, and for him are all things,
Rom. 11:36. But God is altogether for himself, as his highest end, and not
for any others. He is his own end, as well as his own beginning; who never
had a beginning, nor shall ever have an end, Rev. 1:8. As all God doth is for
himself; Rev. 4:11, 'Thou hast created all things, and for thy pleasure they
are and were created;' so all God is, is for himself; he is infinite, wise, almighty, everlasting, unchangeable, holy, righteous, faithful being, is for
himself. It is the profaneness of some men to be somewhat for God, more
for the world, and most of all for their carnal selves. But it is the perfection
of God to be somewhat for the world in general, more for his elect in special, and most of all for himself. Nay, in all that he is for the world or his
elect, he is still most for himself. It is the excellency and purity of saints
and angels to be what they are, and to do what they do, for God, to make
him who is the efficient, the final cause of their beings and actions; but it is
the excellency and purity of God to be what he is, and to do what he doth,
for himself. He who is his own happiness must be his own end.

3. His being is an independent being; he is by himself, as well as from
and for himself; none ever in heaven or earth contributed the least towards
the maintenance or continuance of his being; neither the creatures' goodness nor their goods do him the least good. Not their goodness; men may
be advantaged by the goodness of men, but God cannot: 'My goodness extendeth not to thee, but to the saints that are on earth,' Ps. 16:3. Not their
goods; he is the lord proprietor of the whole world, and if he wanted anything he would not ask the leave of any; for all is his own, but he is above
all want: "If I were hungry, I would not tell thee; for the world is mine, and
the fulness thereof,' Ps. 50:12—i.e., I declare to the world that I am incapable of the least want; or if I needed a meal's meat, I would scorn to go to the
creature's door to beg it. I could supply myself out of my own store, if there

were need; but there is no need at all. He challengeth all the world to produce any being that ever obliged or engaged him in the least: 'Who hath prevented me that I may repay him?' Job 41:11. Where is the man, where is the angel, where is the creature that can say, he ever did me the least kindness, that hath been beforehand with me in courtesy, to whom I am the least in debt for my subsistence? I am here ready to make him amends; 'Who hath prevented me, that I may repay him?'

But all other beings are dependent; the highest, the strongest of them are not able to bear their own weight; but, like the hop or ivy, must have somewhat to lean upon: 'By him all things subsist,' Col. 1:17. He preserveth them in their beings and in their motions: 'In him we live and move, and have our beings,' Acts 17:28. As the beams depend on the sun, and the streams on the fountain, so do the creatures for their beings and actions depend on God. 'He upholdeth all things' (as the foundation the building) 'by the word of his power,' Heb. 1:3. He is the Atlas that bears up the whole world, without whom it would fall to nothing. 'Thou preservest man and beast,' Ps. 36:6. *Dependentia est de essentia creaturæ.*[6]

God is to the world as the soul to the body; he animates and actuates every thing in it, and enableth his several creatures to all their motions. Men are apt to think that fire can burn of itself, it being so natural to the fire to burn; yet if God do but suspend his influence, (*actum secundum*,[7] as they speak) a furnace heated seven times hotter than usual burns no more than water, Dan. 3:27. We are ready to conceive that it is easy for a man to see, when the organ is rightly disposed, there is a fit medium, and a due distance of the organ from the object. But yet, if God deny his concurrence, though there are these three requisites to sight, a man can see no more than if he were stark blind, Gen. 19:11; 2 Kings 6:18.

Angels themselves must have their Maker for their mover; or, as active spirits as they are, they must stand still.

---

[6] "Dependency is of the essence of the creature."
[7] "According to act."

IV

GOD INCOMPARABLE IN HIS BEING, AS HE IS ABSOLUTELY PERFECT, UNIVERSAL, UNCHANGEABLE

4. He is an absolutely perfect being. There is a twofold perfection compatible to beings. Some are perfect in their kind; that is, have all things requisite to that species of which they are. So we say the world is perfect, because it hath all things needful to a world. A man is a perfect man, that hath a body with all its parts and members, and a soul with all its powers and faculties. But secondly, A being is absolutely perfect, when nothing can be added to it, or taken from it, when it is incapable of the least accession or diminution. Now such a being is God, and none but God. As the sun gets nothing by the shining of the moon and the stars, neither loseth anything by their eclipses or withdrawing; so the self-sufficient God gains nothing by all the suits and services, prayers and praises of his creatures; neither loseth anything by their neglect of their duties. He is above the influence of all our performances; our holiness addeth not the least to his happiness: 'Can a man be profitable to God, as he that is wise may be profitable to himself? Is it any pleasure to the Almighty that thou art righteous? Or is it gain to him that thou makest thy ways perfect?' Job 22:2, 3. He is beyond the malice of sin. As holiness doth not help him, so the sin of his creatures doth not hurt him. All those darts of sin which the wicked shoot up against heaven, fall short, and fall down upon their own heads: 'If thou sinnest, what dost thou against him? Or if thy transgressions be multiplied, what dost thou unto him? If thou be righteous, what givest thou him? Or what receiveth he of thine hand? Thy wickedness may hurt a man as thou art; and thy righteousness may profit the sons of men,' Job 35:6–8. Flesh and blood may be injured and pierced by the weapons of unrighteousness; but not the Rock of ages; that is impenetrable. They who are of the same make

and mould with ourselves may be advantaged by our blessings and praises, but not he who is above all blessing and praises.

What doth the great light of the world get by the Persian's admiration and adoration of it? What is a fountain the better if men drink of its water, and commend it; or the worse if men pass by, and despise it? What would God get, if he should make millions of worlds to laud and magnify him? Or what would God lose, if there were no world, no creature at all? 'Who hath given to him, and it shall be recompensed again?' Rom. 11:35. He hath given to all whatever they are, or have; but none ever gave to him. They who give to him their love, and fear, and trust, and names, and estates, give nothing to him. We can give nothing to him, to whom we owe all. Besides, all we have, and are, and do, and suffer for him, addeth nothing to him. His declarative glory may, but his essential glory, or glorious essence, admits not in the least of any increase or decrease. But no other being is absolutely perfect. Men are exceeding imperfect since their fall. They are so far from being above all additions that they stand in continual need of additions. They need the air to breathe in, the earth to bear them, food to strengthen them, raiment to cover them, fire to warm them, sleep to refresh them; they want righteousness to justify them, the Holy Ghost to sanctify them, love to comfort them, and mercy to save them. Man is an heap of infirmities, an hospital of diseases, and a bundle of imperfections. He is so far from being absolutely perfect, that, in a moral consideration, since his apostasy, he is not perfect in his kind. And though angels are more perfect than men, yet they are imperfect to God. Angels, it is true, are perfect in their kind, but not perfect in all kinds; something may be added to them, something may be taken from them. The highest angel may be higher, and the holiest angel may be holier, and the best of them may be better. Though the stars differ from each other in brightness and glory, yet none of them is a sun. Though angels differ from men, and each from others in honour and excellency; yet none of them is a god, none of them is absolutely perfect.

5. God is an universal being, he hath all good eminently and virtually in himself. Whatsoever excellencies are scattered and dispersed among the creatures in heaven or in earth, they are all united in, and centered after an infinite manner in the Creator. It is a true rule in philosophy, *Quod efficit tale est magis tale*, Whatsoever good is in the effect, is more abundantly in the cause. Now God being the principle and cause of all the good and excellency that is in every creature, it must of necessity be more abundantly in

him. As some potions have the quintessence of many herbs, many drugs in them; so God hath the quintessence of all creatures, and infinitely more in him.

For this cause he is called by, and compared to, whatsoever is good and answerable, either to necessity, conveniency, or delight. Sometimes to that good which is necessary; as to life, John 1:4; to the fountain of life, Ps. 36:9; to light, John 1:9; to the Father of lights, James 1:19; to food, as to bread, yea, living bread, John 6:51; to water, yea, living water, John 4:10; to rest, 'Return to thy rest, O my soul, for the Lord hath dealt bountifully with thee,' Ps. 116:7. He is the only ark wherein alone the dove, wearied about the waters of this world, can find rest. Sometimes he is compared to that good which is convenient; as to a habitation, Ps. 90:9, 10; 'O Lord, thou hast been our dwelling-place from all generations.' To health, Ps. 49:11–17; to peace, 2 Cor. 13:11; to protection or defence, as a shield, which defends the body from the shot or thrusts of men, Gen. 15:1; to a wall of fire, which defends the traveller from the fury of beasts, Zech. 2:5; to a refuge, which secures the army, when it is foiled by the enemy, Ps. 57:1; to a rock, a fortress, a high tower, Ps. 18:2; sometimes he is compared to that good which is delightful; as to riches, Job 22:24, 25; to unsearchable riches, Eph. 3:8; durable riches, Prov. 8:18; to honour and glory, as a royal diadem; he is called a glorious Lord, Isa. 33:21; said to be the glory in the midst of his people, Zech. 2:5; to joy and pleasure, Ps. 43:4; to relations, he is a father, 2 Cor. 6:18; an husband, Hosea 2:19; to a feast of fat things, of marrow and fatness, of wine, of wine on the lees well refined, Isa. 25:6; which are the delight of the palate; to beauty, which is the delight of the eyes, Cant. 5:10–16; to sweet smells, which are the delight of the nostrils, Cant. 4:10, and 1:3; to the, most harmonious music, which is the delight of the ears: his mouth is most sweet, or sweetnesses, Cant. 5:16; 'My soul failed when he spake,' so ravishing was his voice, Cant. 5:6; to truth, which is the delight of the understanding, Ps. 31:5; John 14:6; to good, which is the delight of the will, Mat. 19:17. Thus God is not one good, but all good. The truth is, all the good, all the excellencies that are in men or angels, are not worthy to be a shadow, or foil to set off those excellencies that are in God. All good is in one God, Mark 10:29, 30. But creatures are but particular beings. Man is but a particular being, a low limited being: 'What is man, that is a worm; or the son of man, that is a worm?' Job 25:6. There is some good in one man, and some good in another man; but not all good in any man; no, not in all men. Angels are but particular beings, little beings. One angel is one drop, another angel another drop, a third angel a third drop; every one is but a drop. None of them is an ocean, as God is, which containeth all those drops, and infinitely more.

6. God is an unchangeable being, not only without, but incapable of the least alteration. He is the same yesterday, to-day, and forever, Heb. 13:8. He is what he was, and what he will be eternally. He is the same since the world was made that he was before the world, and that he will be when this world shall be no more: 'With him is not the least variation, or shadow of turning,' James 1:17. No παραλλαγὴ, or variableness. It is an astronomical word, taken from the heavenly bodies, which suffer many declensions and revolutions, which they call parallaxes. Though those heavenly lights are variable, have their increases and decreases, their times of rising and setting; yet our Father of lights is not variable. He knoweth no rising or setting, no increasing or decreasing; but shineth always with the same light and lustre, with the same beauty and brightness; nor shadow of turning, τροπῆς ἀποσκίασμα. The lesser luminaries or stars, according to their different postures, have divers shadowings or adumbrations, according to their nearness to, or distance from the sun, their shadows are greater or lesser; but our sun is still the same, knoweth no clouding, no shadowing, no eclipsing. When God hates those angels as apostates, whom first he loved, as created pure and holy, he is still the same; the change is not in God, but in them. Bring clay to the sun, it hardens it; bring wax to the sun, with the same influence, it softens it, without any alteration in the sun. When God punisheth a man that is wicked, and prospereth the same man becoming a penitent, he is still the same. If a man walk on one side of a church, the pillars are on his left hand; if on the other side, on his right hand. The pillars remain where they were, the motion or change is in the man.

But creatures are all mutable; the heavens seem constant, but it is in inconstancy; their perpetual motion speaks their perpetual alteration: Ps. 102:26, 27, 'They shall perish, but thou shalt endure, they shall wax old as a garment,' that is, wearing out, and wasting every day; as a vesture shalt thou change them, and they shall be changed, but thou, Lord, art the same forever.' The old heavens will pass away, and new ones succeed in their room at the general conflagration, but the God of heaven will never pass away. Man is ever in motion, from one condition to another. His body changeth in its age, constitution, temper; at last into rottenness, dust and corruption: 'I have said to corruption, thou art my father; and to the worms, ye are my brother and sister,' Job 17:14. His soul changeth in its passions, affections; love, hatred, delights, desires: his whole man changeth in its place, company, carriage, conversation: he hath no consistency while he is, he continueth not what he was, Job 14:2, 3. Angels are changeable; even the good angels, though not as men, yet as creatures; as perfect as they are, they have this imperfection. 1. They are who once were not, and, in regard of themselves, have a possibility not to be. 2. Angels may lose what they have, and attain what they have not. 3. Angels are mutable in regard of place, sometimes in heaven, sometimes on earth. What little unchangeableness is in angels, is derivative, God is the original of it; their immutability at most is but from their creation, I suppose some time since; for the good angels as well as bad were created mutable, but God's immutability is from eternity. The whole world indeed is a sea of glass, Rev. 4:6, always ebbing and flowing, never at a stay; but the maker of the world may well say, 'I the Lord change not,' Mal. 3:6.

V

GOD INCOMPARABLE IN HIS BEING, AS IT IS
ETERNAL AND WITHOUT COMPOSITION

7. God is an eternal being, and none is eternal but he. Time, which hath a beginning and end, is compatible to men, and other visible creatures in this world. Æviternity, which hath a beginning and no end, is compatible to good and evil angels, and to the souls of men; but eternity, which hath no beginning, succession or end, belongs only to God.

(1). God hath no beginning: he who 'in the beginning created the heavens and the earth,' could have no beginning himself,' Gen. 1:1. 'Before the mountains were brought forth, or ever thou hadst formed the earth and the world; from everlasting to everlasting thou art God,' Ps. 90:2. God is eternal, a parte ante, and puzzleth most enlarged understanding to conceive his duration. 'Behold he is great, and we know him not, neither can the number of his years be searched out,' Job 36:26, Ps. 93:2.

(2). God hath no succession in his duration; he dwelleth in one indivisible point of eternity; he is what he is in one infinite moment of being; his duration knoweth nothing of former or latter, past or to come; his essence is not bounded by those hedges, but he enjoyeth his whole eternity every moment; hence he is said to 'inhabit eternity,' to be fixed always in eternity, Isa. 57:15. Time is *nunc fluens*,[8] but eternity is *nunc stans*[9]: 'One day with him is as a thousand years, and a thousand years as one day,' 2 Pet. 3:8. He inhabits a million of years in a moment, and each moment to him is as a million of years. He hath not the least added to his duration since the world was, though it hath been near six thousand years: it is not proper to say of him, he was, for none of his duration is ever past with him, or he shall be, for none of his duration is ever to come; but he is, his full eternity is always present, hence his name is I Am, Exod. 3:14. Not I was, or shall be;

---

[8] "Now flowing."
[9] "Now standing still."

and Christ tells the Jews, 'Before Abraham was, I Am,' John 8:58. It seems false grammar, but it is the most proper true divinity. Indeed, had Adam been then alive, it had been proper for him to have said, before Abraham was, I was; or if an angel had spoken, it had been proper for him to have said, before Abraham was, I was; because men and angels enjoy their being by piecemeals, now a little and then a little, somewhat of their duration is gone, and somewhat to come; but it was most proper for him that was God to say, before Abraham was, I Am, because his duration is without all succession, the whole of it is ever present. The psalmist further clears this, 'Thou art my son, this day have I begotten thee,' Ps. 2:7; which words are interpreted of the eternal generation of the Son of God before all worlds, and also of his resurrection in time, which was to be some hundreds of years after, as the apostle either expounds it, or alludes to it, Acts 13:33. But it is all one, for both are to-day; that which was from eternity, and that which was to be many hundred of years after, are both with him present this day.

Past or future is all present this day; that was not past to God which never had beginning, his son's eternal generation; nor was that to come to God which was always before him, his son's temporal resurrection. It is still, 'This day have I begotten thee;' millions of years, yea, of ages, add not the least moment to his duration.

(3). God hath no ending: as he is from, so he is to everlasting, Ps. 90:2. 'Without beginning or end of days,' Ps. 102:27. 'But thou art the same, and thy years never end.' O what an excellent being is this eternal being? 'He only hath immortality,' 1 Tim. 6:16. And he is eternity itself, 1 Sam. 15:29. *Æternitas Israelis*, Jun. The eternity of Israel cannot lie.

But are men or angels comparable to God in this? Surely no. As for man, he is a bird of time, here to-day and gone tomorrow, Job 14:1. Of few days: 'As for man, his days are as grass,' Ps. 103:5; now flourishing, but quickly perishing.

Man hath a beginning, succession, and ending. There was a time when man was not; man enjoyeth his time by parts and parcels, and man ere long shall be no more. All men in this are alike, high or low, good or bad. There is a vast difference between God and all men in their duration. 'Are thy days as the days of man? Are thy years as man's years?' Job 10:5. No, in no respect. Man's days begin, succeed, and end; not so God's days. Well might David say, though he had lived as long as Methusaleh, 'Mine age is nothing unto thee,' Ps. 39:5. And truly as men are far from being comparable to God, so are angels. Angels had a beginning, Col. 1:16. Angels have a succession in their duration; they enjoy part to-day, part to-morrow, part the next day; every moment addeth to their duration; what is past they do not enjoy, nor what is to come, but only what is present; and thus it is also with souls of saints in heaven.

8. God is a simple being. In this I take simplicity, not as opposed to wisdom, for in him are all the treasures of wisdom and knowledge, Col. 2:9, but as simplicity is opposed to mixture and composition. Thus there is a simplicity in the gospel, 2 Cor. 12:3. So anything, the more simple it is, the more excellent it is. God is a most pure, simple, unmixed, indivisible essence; he is incapable of the least composition, and therefore of the least division. He is one most pure, one without all parts, members, accidents, and qualities. Whatsoever is in him is himself, his very being; therefore, that which is a quality in a man or angel, is attributed to God in the abstract. Men and angels are wise, but God is wisdom, Prov. 9:1. Men and angels are holy, but God is holiness, Isa. 63:15. God is all essence, all being, and nothing else.

But how unlike are men or angels to God in this! Man is a grossly compounded being; he is compounded of a body and a soul, Gen. 2:7. His body is compounded of members and parts; his members and parts are compounded of bones, and blood, and flesh, and skin, and sinews, Job 10:11. His soul is compounded, and so are the highest angels, of substance and accidents, of essence and faculties; the substance of man's soul, and of angels and their qualities, are distinct things. Their wisdom is one thing, their power another thing, their holiness a third thing, and all distinct from their essence. An angel may be an angel, and a man may be a true man, and yet be foolish, weak, and wicked. Their understanding differeth from their wills, their wills differ from their affections, their affections differ from both, and all from their beings. But in God all these are one indivisible essence, to will and to understand, and to love and to hate, and to be, are all the same and one in God.

VI

GOD INCOMPARABLE IN HIS BEING, AS IT IS INFINITE AND INCOMPREHENSIBLE

9. God is an infinite being. He is a being that knoweth no bounds, no limits. His being is without all measure, all degrees and determinations. His understanding, i.e., himself, who is all understanding, is infinite, Ps. 147:5. God is a sphere, whose centre is everywhere, and whose circumference is nowhere. 'Behold the heavens, and heaven of heavens cannot contain thee, how much less this house which I have built,' 1 Kings 8:27. The starry heavens, or firmament, is large; it compasseth the whole earth and ocean; this terrestrial world is but a point to it; but the heaven of heavens, or the imperial heaven, is larger; it containeth the lower heaven, but cannot contain the God of heaven. No ubi, no place can define or circumscribe him. He is neither shut up in any place nor shut out of any place. He is above place, without place, yet in all places. 'Whither shall I go from thy Spirit? Or whither shall I flee from thy presence? If I ascend up into heaven, thou art there; if I make my bed in hell, (heaven and hell are most opposite places,) behold thou art there. If I take the wings of the morning, and dwell in the uttermost parts of the sea, even there shall thy hand lead me, and thy right hand shall hold me,' Ps. 139:7–10. God is in heaven, earth, sea, hell, and infinitely more, where there is neither heaven, nor earth, nor sea, nor hell.

Oh, what a being is the blessed God, who is boundless not only in his duration, of which we have spoken before, and in all his perfections and attributes, of which we shall speak hereafter, but also in his essence and being! No place can circumscribe him, and no *ubi*[10] can define him. 'He is over all' creatures by his power and dominion; 'in you all,' by his essence and influence; 'and through all,' by his providence, Eph. 4:6. He is everywhere, not only virtually, as the sun by his beams; nor authoritatively, as a king by subordinate officers; not at all by multiplication, as the loaves filled

---

[10] "Where."

that place, which they did not before the miracle; or by extension, as the rational creature filleth that place when a man, which he did not when an infant; nor by local motion, from one place to another, as all bodily animate creatures; or by division, as our bodies are part in one place and part in another; or by commixtion, as the air mingleth itself with the terrestrial world; but essentially after an unspeakable manner. As philosophers say of the soul, it is whole in the whole body, and whole in every part of the body; so I may say of God, he is whole in the whole world, and whole in every part of the world; yea, if he should please to make ten thousand worlds, he would fill all, and his whole essence be in every part of each world, and yet without the least extension, or multiplication, or motion.

But are men or angels like to God in this? Alas, they are finite, limited beings, less than drops to this ocean. Man is in a small place, so as to fill it up by commensuration of parts, and to exclude all other bodies; but himself is circumscribed in it. Angels, though they are not in a place so as to exclude bodies, yet they are in a *ubi*,[11] or space, so as to conclude themselves therein; they are in a finite compass, beyond which their being extendeth not; they are so here that they are not there; so in heaven that they are not on earth at the same time. But God is everywhere in his whole essence every moment; 'he filleth all in all,' Eph. 1:23.

10. God is an incomprehensible being, such a being as no creature, whether man or angel, can comprehend or perfectly understand. This floweth from the former; if he be infinite, he must of necessity be incomprehensible; for a finite being, as all are beside himself, can never comprehend what is infinite. There is no proportion between a boundless being and a bounded understanding. But there must be a proportion between the mind of the creature and that object which is fully understood by it. The sun may be contained in a small chink, and the sea in a nut-shell, sooner than God can be contained in the limited understanding of men or angels: Job 26:14, 'Lo, these are parts of his ways,' viz., 'hell is naked before him,' ver. 6. 'He hangeth the earth upon nothing,' ver. 7. 'He bindeth up the waters in his thick clouds, and the cloud is not rent under them,' ver. 8. 'He hath compassed the waters with bounds,' ver. 10. 'The pillars of heaven tremble at his reproof,' ver. 11, &c.; 'but how little a portion is heard of him!' The vulgar read it, how little a drop; others, a whisper, or smallest part of a voice; that which is known of God, to that which God is, and is in

---

[11] "Where" or "place."

God, is but like a drop to the vast ocean, and as a whisper to a loud terrible thunder. 'How little a portion is heard of him.' Surely much is heard of him, from the voice of his almighty works of creation and providence, and especially from the voice of his word and his own mouth in the Holy Scriptures. But how little is heard of him in comparison of that immense excellency which is in him, and which he is. Heathens hear somewhat of him, Rom. 1:20, 21. His saints on earth hear much more of him, Ps. 63:3–6. Perfect spirits in heaven hear most of all of him, 2 Cor. 12:3, 4; 1 Cor. 13:12. Yet by all these a very little portion is heard of him.

The being of God is like the peace of God, 'which passeth all understanding,' Phil. 4:7. And like the love of Christ, 'which passeth all knowledge,' Eph. 3:19. This only can be known of God, that he can never be known fully; and this only can be comprehended of him, that he cannot be comprehended: 'Canst thou by searching find out God? Canst thou find out the Almighty to perfection? It is as high as heaven, what canst thou do? Deeper than hell, what canst thou know? The measure thereof is longer than the earth, and broader than the sea,' Job 11:8, 9. 'Canst thou by searching find out God?' It is a strong negation, i.e., it is impossible by all the help and advantage of nature and art, and grace and diligence, yea, and perfect glory too, to find out God fully. Dost thou, a poor mean vile man, saith Zophar, think to contain and comprehend him, whom the heavens, and heaven of heavens, cannot contain or comprehend? Art thou so silly as to conceive that the short line of thy understanding should fathom his bottomless being? It is not in vain for thee to seek him, but it is altogether in vain for thee to search him. Though he be not far from thee, yet he is far above thee, and far beyond thee; far above thy thoughts, and beyond thy conceptions: he 'dwelleth in that light that is inaccessible, whom no man hath seen, nor can see,' 1 Tim. 6:16. They who see him face to face, i.e., most clearly and fully, see but little of him; clouds and darkness are in this sense ever about him. As in a dark clay we see the beams, but not the body of the sun; so even in heaven the highest angels rather see his rays and beams than his infinite being.

'Canst thou find out the Almighty to perfection?' Men who seek God may find him, Prov. 8:17; Mat. 7:7; but they cannot find him to perfection: the word for perfection signifieth the height or utmost accomplishment of a thing. Somewhat of God may be known, but not all; they who find out most are far from finding out the utmost of him. The sun and all the celestial lights may sooner be grasped in the hollow of man's hand, and the vast hills and mountains weighed in a pair of common scales, than the Almighty 'found out to perfection.' Natural questions soon pose the most learned men; the forms even of inanimate creatures are riddles to most. How frequently do the greatest scholars betake themselves to secret sympathies and antipathies, and occult qualities, as the cloak and cover of their ignorance: Eccles. 11:5. 'Canst thou know how the bones grow of her that is with child? O how much more must divine questions exceed human understanding.

'It is as high as heaven, what canst thou do?' It is as the highnesses of heaven: take all the heights and elevations, all the spheres and altitudes of heaven, and try if thou canst reach them with thy short arm; yea, climb up the highest storeys, the loftiest pinnacles, touch, if thou canst, the several orbs; yet the knowledge of this God, or this God the object of knowledge, is above and beyond all. What a fool would he be thought, who should undertake to ascend the starry heavens; yet he who would find out God to perfection, must climb much higher. The heavens are famous for their height; yea, the starry heavens, that some wonder that the eyes of man are not tired before they reach them, Prov. 25:3, 'The heavens for height, and the earth for depth,' yet the third heavens are much higher than they; but the most high God is far higher than the highest heavens.

'Deeper than hell, what canst thou know?' Heaven and hell are at the greatest distance, and are most remote from our apprehensions. Who knoweth what is done in heaven? What in hell? What is enjoyed in the one, or suffered in the other? No more can any know what God is. Who knoweth the nature, number, order, motions, influence of the heavenly bodies; something is conjecturally delivered about them, nothing certain; much less doth any know the number, nature, order, wonder, worship of the celestial courtiers in the third heavens, of the thousand thousand that are before God, the ten thousand times ten thousand that minister to him; least of all can any know that being that made all these, that preserveth all these, that ordereth and governeth, animateth and actuateth all these; that gives them all that they are, and enableth them to all that they do.

'Deeper than hell, what canst thou know?' Who knoweth the mines and minerals which lie in the bosom, in the bowels of the earth? Who knoweth the place of sapphires, the coral, the pearls, and the precious onyx? Job 28:5-8. 'Out of the earth cometh bread, &c. The stones of it are the place of sapphires, and it hath dust of gold. There is a path which no fowl knoweth, and which the vulture's eye hath not seen: the lion's whelps have not trodden it, nor the fierce lion passed by it.' Much less doth any know the miseries of the damned, the extremity, universality, eternity of their torments. Who ever returned from that place, to tell us what they suffered there; or if they had, whose understanding is large enough to conceive them? 'Who knoweth the power of thine anger? According to thy fear, so is thy wrath,' Ps. 90:11. Least of all can any know that God, who setteth an end to darkness, and searcheth out all perfection; the stones of darkness and the shadow of death, Job 28:3: before whom hell and destruction are naked and open; who formeth the costly jewels, secret from the eyes of covetous mortals, who layeth the dark vault of hell, and storeth it with fire and brimstone, and gnawing worms, and blackness of darkness, and all the instruments of eternal death.

'The measure thereof is longer than the earth:' the earth is long, from one end of it to another. Mathematicians tell us, from east to west, it is twenty-two thousand miles, but the knowledge of God is much longer; the measure thereof is beyond all measure.

'And broader than the sea:' the ocean is exceeding broad, it seems to them that sail on it to be without banks or bounds. Hence we read of the arms of the sea, Dan. 11:22, because of its breadth. And David calls it, Ps. 104:25, a great and wide sea; 'So is this great and wide sea wherein are things innumerable, both small and great.' But the knowledge of the great God is far greater and wider: how are the dimensions of height, depth, length and breadth, in their greatest extent and dimensions, obvious to human understandings? The heavens are high, yet their height is finite: hell is deep, yet its depth is determined; the earth is long, yet its length is limited; the sea is broad, yet its breadth is bounded: but God is infinite, boundless, and beyond all these.

VII

GOD INCOMPARABLE IN HIS ATTRIBUTES, IN HIS HOLINESS, AND WISDOM

II. God is incomparable, as in his being, so in his attributes. The attributes of God are those perfections in the divine nature which are ascribed to him, that we might the better understand him. They are so called, i.e., attributes, because they are attributed to him for our sakes, though they are not in him as they are in men or angels. *Vocantur attributa, quia ea sibi attribuit Deus nostra causa,* Zanch de Attribut., lib. ii. cap. 12.[12] *Attributa Dei dicuntur quæ Deo adscribuntur in Scripturis sacris, non tam ad essentiam naturamque Dei explicandam, quam ad declarandum nobis aliquo modo pro nostro captu illud quod de ipso a nobis cognosci potest,* Polan Syntag., lib. ii. cap. 6.[13] There are some attributes of God which the schoolmen call incommunicable, (which I have spoken of under the former head,) because the creature, as a creature, is uncapable of them, and therefore they cannot be attributed to man or angels. It is impossible for a creature to be independent, selfsufficient, eternal in a strict sense, infinite, &c., so that all will acknowledge God incomparable in those excellencies. There are other attributes of God which are called communicable, viz., his power, holiness, wisdom, faithfulness, &c., because they are communicated by him to his rational creatures, and there is some show or shadow of them in men

---

[12] "They are called attributes, because God attributes them to Himself for our sake," in *Dei Natura Dei, Seu De Divinis Attributis* (Concerning the Nature of God, or Concerning the Divine Attributes) by Italian reformer, Girolamo Zanchi (1516-1519).

[13] "The attributes of God are spoken of, which are ascribed to God in the sacred Scriptures, not so much to explain the essence and nature of God, as to declare to us by some mode on behalf of our capacity that which is able to be understood by us concerning himself," in *Syntagma Theologiae Christianae* (An Orderly Arrangement of Christian Theology), by Amandus Polanus von Polansdorf (1561-1610).

and angels. For though it was the horrible pride, and monstrous presumption of evil angels, and Adam, at first to rival God in his properties that were incommunicable—to aspire to be like him in his independency and sovereignty; for their sin was, that they would have cut off the entail, and have held all of themselves, as their own lords and masters; and the Prince of Tyre, Ezek. 28:6, is indicted by God of inexpiable arrogancy, 'that he durst set his heart as the heart of God:' yet it is the only godliness of the creature to be like God, in those attributes of his which are communicable. The new man is after God, Eph. 4:24, the re-impression of his image on the creature. David is therefore called a man after God's own heart, because he was a man after God's own holiness; yea, it is the perfection and felicity of the intellectual world (Ps. 17:15; 1 John 3:3, 4) in heaven.

But even in these properties wherein man resembleth his Maker, he is exceedingly unlike him, and falls infinitely short of him. That God is incomparable in his communicable attributes, I shall discover—1. More generally; 2. More specially.

1. More generally; and here I shall enumerate some of those attributes wherein men and angels are conformable to God, and in each of them shew that in those in which they come nearest to him, they come far behind.

(1). He is incomparable in his holiness. Holiness in general is the moral goodness of a thing, or its conveniency or agreement with its rule. Holiness in the creatures is their conformity to the will of their Creator in the principle, rule, and end of their actions and motions. Holiness in God is that excellency of the divine nature by which he acteth from himself, for himself, and according to his own will.

God is the holy One, Hosea 11:9, by way of eminency and excellency, because he surpasseth all others in holiness. He is the holy One of Jacob, Isa. 49:23; the holy One of Israel, Isa. 43:14, because of their special interest and propriety in the excellent being. He is 'holy, holy, holy,' Isa. 6:3; Rev. 4:8. His nature is the only pattern of holiness, therefore he commands us to look on him as our example: 'Be ye holy as I am holy,' 1 Pet. 1:15, 16. Man was made holy, Eccles. 7:29, i.e., according to the image of God, Gen. 1:26; Eph. 4:24. His will is the only rule of holiness. Hence our holiness is called a proving his good and perfect and acceptable will, Rom. 12:2, and our fulfilling the will of God, Acts 13; and a walking according to his word, which is his revealed will, as our rule, Gal. 6:16. He is universally holy in his name, Luke 1:49; in his nature, Ps. 5:5, 6; Hab. 1:13; in his works, Ps. 145:17; in his word, Rom. 7:12; Ps. 119:140. He is the original of all holiness in men or angels; they are beholden to him that they are not as unholy as the damned, as the devils, James 1:17; Ezek. 37:28, and 38:16, 17; 1 Thes. 5:23. Now what man or angel is comparable to him in holiness? May I not with Moses make a challenge—'Who is a god like unto thee, glorious in holiness?' Exod. 15:11.

Are men holy as he is holy? Nay, are the spirits of just men made perfect, and angels, equal to him in holiness? 'Behold, he putteth no trust in his saints, (the best on earth;) the heavens (the holiest there) are unclean in his sight,' Job 15:15, 16. As for man, he is a sink of sin, a sty of filth, overspread from head to foot with the leprosy of sin, Gen. 6:5; and therefore, instead of comparing with God for holiness, is bound to abhor himself for his unholiness; yea, angels, who have nothing amiss in their natures, who never took one step awry in their lives, who have ever continued God's loyal subjects and faithful servants, observant of all his calls, and obedient to all his commands—whose obedience to him, and observance of him, is made the copy for us to write after, Mat. 6:10—are yet unholy in comparison of God. 'The heavens are unclean in his sight.' The heavens, not only the place, which hath a relative holiness, in regard of God's special presence; but even the persons in heaven, perfect spirits, who have no blemish in their beings, or disorder in their motions, are unholy to him, and unclean in his sight. The holiness of angels is but the holiness of obeying a law, Ps. 103:20, 21; the holiness of God is the holiness of being a law, 1 Thes. 4:3. The holiness of angels is but a conformity to the pattern set them; the holiness of God is the holiness of setting them a pattern, and of being their pattern. The holiness of angels is but a derivative, God's is an original holiness.

God is so incomparable in holiness that it is said, he only, or solely, is holy, Rev. 15:4, 'Who will not fear thee, O Lord, and glorify thy name? For thou only art holy.' None is holy besides him, because none is holy like him; 1 Sam. 2:2, 'There is none holy as the Lord,' therefore none holy but the Lord: saints are holy, 1 Pet. 2:9; angels are holy, Mark 8:38; but they are not holy as the Lord is holy. Without question, the heavenly host, who see him face to face, and are satisfied with his likeness, are glorious in holiness, shine brightly with those perfect beams, and that pure light which they borrow from the Sun of righteousness; but truly they are poor glow-worms to the Father of lights. Even that grace, that holiness, that glory of saints and angels which infinitely surpasseth the natural heavens in all their beauty and brightness, is no grace, no holiness, no glory in this respect, by reason of that grace and holiness and glory in God, which doth so infinitely excel.

(2). God is incomparable in his wisdom, (I shall not stand upon the critical distinctions which some give between understanding, prudence, and wisdom) wisdom in general is a right understanding of things, and the ordering ourselves and actions suitable to that understanding. It appears chiefly in these three acts: 1. In discerning the nature, causes, effects, contraries, and consequents of things, (of which we shall speak hereafter;) and this we call science. 2. In propounding the best, and highest, and noblest end to ourselves in our actions and undertakings; and this is called understanding. 3. In suiting and fitting and ordering the most proper means as may be best for the attaining our ends; and this is called prudence, which, as the rudder of the ship, steers and directs and governs all. In all these respects God is incomparable in wisdom: 'he is wise in heart,' Job 9:4, i.e., most wise; for the heart is the seat of wisdom; and to be foolish, and without an heart, is all one: 'Ephraim is a silly dove, without a heart,' Hosea 7:11. There are in God 'all the treasures of wisdom,' Col. 1:19.

A treasure denotes, 1. Preciousness; a heap of dust or coals is not a treasure, but of silver and gold. 2. Plenty; one or two pieces of things that are precious will not make a treasure, there must be a heap, or some quantity. In God there is the most precious wisdom, therefore called counsel, the effect of serious and mature deliberation; and he is called the Mighty Counsellor, Eph. 1:11; Isa. 9:6. In God there is plenty of it, treasures; a treasure notes abundance, but treasures speak superabundance, a redundance. In God are all the treasures, all kinds, all sorts of wisdom, τολυποίκιλος σοφία, manifold wisdom, Eph. 3:10, embroidered wisdom, wherein is all variety of rich and curious contrivances. These are all in God; he engrosseth them all in himself; therefore you read, 'With him is wisdom and understanding,' Job 12:13; with him, as with its master and sovereign lord; with him, as with its sole owner and proprietor.

Some men are wise; light and understanding, and excellent wisdom, was found in Daniel, Dan. 5:14. David was very wise, wiser than his teachers, than his enemies, than the ancient, Ps. 119:97–99. Solomon was a wise man, he exceeded in wisdom all that were before, and all that came after him: 'And God gave Solomon wisdom and understanding exceeding much, and largeness of heart, even as the sand on the sea-shore; and Solomon's wisdom excelled the wisdom of all the children of the east country, and all the wisdom of Egypt, for he was wiser than all men, than Ethan and Heman,' &c., 1 Kings 4:29–31. But was Solomon comparable to God in wisdom? Truly, he that was wiser than all men was a stark fool to God; the wisdom of man is foolishness with God, 1 Cor. 3:19. The subtilty of the heathen, and, I may say, the greatest understanding of the Christian, is folly with God: 'The foolishness of God is wiser than man,' 1 Cor. 1:25. If it were possible that there should be anything in God which might look like folly, or if it were lawful for us to conceive any action of God's, which, compared with his deeper contrivances, might have a show of foolishness, yet even this were wiser than the greatest wisdom of man. Angels are wiser than men. When the woman would speak David to be very wise above the rate of mortals, she saith, 'My lord is wise as an angel of God,' 2 Sam. 14:20. The excellency of their natures speaks the excellency of their wisdom, for it is the understanding that is the chief distinguishing faculty. But are angels like God in wisdom? No, they are fools to him: 'Behold, he putteth no trust in his servants, he chargeth his angels with folly,' Job 4:18. Though they never thwarted the divine pleasure, nor in any action manifested the least imprudence; yet before him they are indicted of folly, and to him will be proved guilty of it. Though they are not chargeable with actual, yet they are with potential folly; though God doth not indict them of absolute, yet he doth of comparative folly.

God doth so far exceed angels and men in wisdom that he is said only to be wise: 'To the only wise God,' 1 Tim. 1:17; To God only wise,' Rom. 16:27. None are wise beside him, because none are wise to him, Dan. 5:20. Wisdom is his, his peculiar, his prerogative, his wholly, his only; so his that it is none's but his.

The wisest men and angels stand in need of a master to teach them, and a tutor to instruct them; and were it not for the only wise God, they would be as unwise as the wild ass's colt, as foolish as idiots, Ps. 94:10. But God is above all teachers, all tutors, Job 21:22, 'Shall any teach God knowledge?' Some persons are incapable of teaching because of their extreme weakness; *Ex quovis ligno non fit Mercurius*,[14] their parts are so very low and mean, that they cannot be taught. But God is incapable of teaching, because of his immense wisdom; his abilities are so high that they are above and beyond all instruction: Isa. 40:13, 14, 'Who hath directed the Spirit of the Lord, or being his counsellor, hath taught him?' The wise Solomon had his privy counsellors, the wisest princes and states have their council—tables, and there is reason enough for it, because two heads are better than one, as we say, and two eyes see more than one: 'Two are better than one,' Eccles. 6:9;

---

[14] "Mercury was not made from any block of wood" variously attributed to Horace or Pythagoras.

and in many counsellors there is safety. But God, who is all head, all eye, all understanding, needs none to advise or counsel him. Two candles indeed are better than one, because the light of each is little and small, and capable of increase, but one sun is better than a million of candles, because its light is, after a sort, boundless, and incapable of the least addition or increase by millions of candles. Ver. 14. 'With whom took he counsel?' with what angel, with what man, with what politician did he ever consult? Who instructed him in the paths of judgment? Taught him what was just, what was unjust, what to do, what to forbear? How to govern and order the affairs of the world, in what manner and measure to cut out and carve every one's portion? Who taught him knowledge, and shewed him the way of understanding? Where is the creature that can say he obliged God by giving him directions in any case? Where is the man, the angel, that can speak it, that he ever taught God one lesson, or told him one letter? If any such be, God will pay him well for his learning: Rom. 11:34, 35, 'Who hath known the mind of the Lord? Or who hath been his counsellor? Who hath given to him, and it shall be recompensed to him again?' We may know the mind of God for our instruction, but we can never know the mind of God for his instruction, 1 Cor. 2:16.

(3). God is incomparable in his power. Power is that ability or force by which we act. Power in God is that attribute by which he effecteth whatsoever he pleaseth. In this he hath no equal: 'Who is a strong God like unto thee?' Ps. 89:8. Where is the being that is like him in strength? God is not only strong, but mighty in strength, Job 9:4; not only powerful, but excellent in power, Job 37:23. Job hath a notable expression: chap. 9:19, 'If I speak of strength, lo he is strong'—i.e., as it is ordinary with us, when we would lift a man up to the height of praise for, any quality in him, to say, If you speak of wealth, there is a rich man; if you speak of learning, there is a scholar for you; so here saith Job, 'If I speak of strength, lo he is strong.' If I speak of strength and ability to contend and fight, lo, behold, wonder, here is one that is strong indeed, that never contendeth but he prevaileth; who never combats but he conquers: he is strong indeed; he is strong to purpose, with effect. He can offend, and there is no standing before him: Dan. 4:35, he doth whatsoever he will, and none can stay his hand. He can stop the motion of the strongest creature in its fullest, swiftest career, but none can stop or stay him in his actions. Many have presumption enough to oppose him, but none have power enough to overcome him. He can defend, and there is no striving with him: Isa. 43:2, 'When thou passest through the waters (be they never so boisterous, so tempestuous, so deep, so danger-ous) I will be with thee, and they shall not overflow thee.' The floods of the ungodly may be very fierce and violent, but they shall never overflow, or overcome, those whom God is pleased to protect. It must be a strange and strong arrow that can pierce such a shield of defence, Gen. 15:1.

David tells us, 'God hath spoken once, yea twice have I heard thee,' Ps. 62:11. It was some special extraordinary thing certainly that David ushers in with such a preface, that God spake so solemnly, and he heard so atten-tively. But what was it? 'That power belongeth to God' as his proper pecu-liar excellency, as his crown and sceptre.

God is not only mighty, but almighty; not only the mighty God, Isa. 9:6, but the almighty God, 2 Cor. 6:18. He is a God that never met with a diffi-culty, much less with an impossibility. Nothing is too hard for God, Gen. 18:14. All things are hard to men, and many things too hard for men or an-gels, but nothing is too hard for God: 'I know that thou canst do all things,' Job 42:2.

Men are strong: they may have a natural strength as men, a civil strength as magistrates; they may be too strong in themselves for other persons, and too strong in their armies and militias for other kingdoms and countries; but are they strong enough for God? Surely no: 1 Cor. 1:25, The weakness of God is stronger than man: *Ubi Deus virtutem suam occultando infirmiter agere videtur, robustior tamen illa quæ putatur imbecillitas, quavis hominum virtute.*—Calv. in Corinth.[15] Not that there is any weak-ness in God—for should any think so, he ungods him—but in those actions wherein God is pleased to conceal his power, and seemeth to act infirmly; even that seeming infirmity excels all human power and strength. Hence it is that God throweth down the gauntlet to Job: Job 40:9, 'Hast thou an arm like God?' By arm is meant power and strength, because the arm is that member of man by which he exerteth and exerciseth that power and strength which he hath; so Job 35:9; i.e., Job, though thou hast had a strong natural arm, and a strong civil arm, as the greatest man in the east, and a king in the army, Job 1:3, 29:25, yet hast thou an arm like God? Canst thou make and unmake, kill and make alive, cast down and lift up at thy pleas-ure, as I do? Is thine arm as long to reach all thine enemies, and as strong

---

[15] "While God appears to act with weakness, in consequence of his concealing his power, that weakness, as it is reckoned, is stronger than any power of men," from John Calvin's commentary on 1 Corinthians 1:25.

to break and bruise them in pieces with a blow? Hast thou an arm like God? Canst thou brandish and wield a sword with thine arm to the terror and horror, to the confusion and destruction of all that oppose thee? 'God hath a mighty arm, strong is his hand, high is his right hand,' Ps. 89:13.

Angels are stronger than men. The evil angel is called the strong man, Luke 11:21; they are styled principalities and powers, Eph. 6:12; roaring lions, 1 Pet. 5:8; red dragons, Rev. 12:9; which denote their power to be far superior to man's. The devil is the prince of the powers of the air, Eph. 2:2; can command storms and tempests, and with a puff of his mouth blow down houses and cities. Good angels probably are stronger; one of them in a night destroyeth 184,000 men. They are so strong that they are said to excel in strength, Ps. 103:20. And indeed the spirituality and purity of their natures speaks their power. Man's weakness is partly from his flesh, which is a phrase whereby the prophet describes the impotency of the creature: 'They are men, and their horses are flesh, and not spirit,' Isa. 31:3. And when the Holy Ghost would describe the strength of a thing, he opposeth it to flesh, 2 Cor. 10:4: 'Our weapons are not fleshly or carnal, but mighty,' partly from his moral filthiness, his sin, which, being a real disease, doth debilitate and weaken the powers of man. Hence, to be a sinner, and to be without strength, is all one, Rom. 5:6, 8, and holiness is called the strength of man, Rev. 3:8. But angels are spirits, not flesh: 'He maketh his angels spirits,' Ps. 104:4. And good angels are free from sin, therefore called holy angels, Mark 8:38. Yet notwithstanding all their power as spirits, as sinless spirits, they are weakness to God. As it is said of leviathan, 'He esteemeth iron as straw, and brass as rotten wood,' Job 41:27: so I may say of God; he esteemeth the strength of evil angels as straw, and of good angels as rotten wood. Evil angels are fettered, wherever they go, in the chains of his anger and his power, which they cannot break asunder, but must bear, as intolerable as they are. And good angels own and acknowledge his might and strength above all other, Rev. 4:8, 11. The power of God hath no fellow, no parallel. There is no rock, i.e., no strength, rocks being strong natural fortifications; Vide 1 Sam. 14:4; Judges 6:16, like our God, 1 Sam. 2:2.

(4). God is incomparable in his justice. Justice in general is the giving every one their due. In God, it is that attribute whereby he disposeth all things according to the rule of equity, Deut. 32:4; Ps. 11:5; and rendereth to every man according to his works, without respect of persons, Ps. 62:12; Job 34:11, 19; Gal. 6:6, 7. God is positively or affirmatively just: Zeph. 3:5, 'The just Lord is in the midst thereof, he will not do iniquity.' He is eminently the just one, Acts 7:52; he is superlatively most just, Job 34:17. Wilt thou condemn him that is most just? Altogether just; or, as some read it, justice justice, without the least mixture, tincture, or shadow of injustice; all over just and justice. He is most just, just in the highest degree, just beyond all degrees. He giveth to all their due, without fear of evil—he standeth in awe of none for their power or greatness; his day of vengeance is against the cedars of Lebanon, and the oaks of Bashan, and all the high mountains, Isa. 2:13, 14—without hope of gain; men are unjust for bribes, Hosea 4:14, and love with shame give ye; but riches prevail not in the day of his wrath, Prov. 11:4; Ezek. 7:19. He is no taker of gifts, 2 Chron. 19:7, and without respect to any, for their nearness or relation to him, or honours, or outward excellencies, Jer. 22:24. He will pluck the signet from his right hand in the day of his justice. Israel were a people near to him, Deut. 4:7; Ps. 148:14, yet he doth not spare them when they rebel against him, Ps. 76:1-3, 44:10-15; Jer. 7:12. Read the Lamentations of Jeremiah, and you will find his severity to them, notwithstanding their near relation to him. Adam and angels were great and excellent beings, yet when they sinned, he made them to suffer: 'He accepteth not the persons of princes, nor regardeth the rich more than the poor,' Job 34:19. He acteth according to law most exactly, and according to a law published, and according to a most righteous and just law, Rom. 2:12, 13, 15, 16, and 7:12, therefore is most just: 'Surely God will not do wickedly, neither will the Almighty pervert judgment,' Job 34:12. Surely the Almighty cannot do wickedly, neither can God pervert judgment. Men may do justly, God must do justly; he cannot but do justly; and that because his will is his law, and the most exact platform and rule of all justice and righteousness. Whatsoever he doth is just, because he doth it who is the great sovereign and supreme of the world, Job 34:12, 13.

The actions of God are often mysterious, but ever righteous: Ps.145:17, 'The Lord is holy in all his ways, and righteous in all his works.' When his paths are in the seas, and his goings in deep waters, Ps. 77:19, that none can fathom them, or find out the reason of them, even then all his ways are judgment, Deut. 32:4. Not as judgment is opposed to mercy, but as judgment is opposed to injustice. 'When clouds and darkness are before him,' i.e., when his providences are such hard texts that none can expound them, and such dark riddles that none can unfold them; even then, 'righteousness and judgment are the habitation of his throne,' Ps. 99:2. His disposing and distributive power moves always within the sphere of righteousness.

Men may be just, Mat. 1:19; Joseph was a just man; Noah, Gen. 6:9; John, Mark 6:20; Cornelius, Acts 10:22. 'But shall mortal man be more just than God? Shall man be more pure than his Maker?' Job 4:17. The expression is a denial of all comparison between God and man: it is the highest presumption for man to prefer himself before God, Isa. 14:13, 14. Yea, it is monstrous impudency for man to compare himself with God. We say amongst men that comparisons are odious; but this is the most odious comparison of all, for Enosh, a weak frail creature, to compare with Elohah, the mighty, almighty Creator; for crookedness to compare with straightness, and darkness to compare with light. The most just man compared with God is unjust; his righteousness is as a filthy rag: 'In his sight can no flesh be justified,' Ps. 143:2. Though in the sight of men a man may be just, yet in the sight of God he is unjust. Compare a star with a candle, and it is somewhat; but compare it with the sun, and it is nothing—it must hide its head for shame. Compare a godly man with a wicked man, or one not so good as himself, and he is somebody; but compare him with an angel, he is nobody: what is he then, if he be compared with a God? Job 9:2, 3: 'How should man be just with God?' Speak the way, declare the means, the manner, how man should be righteous before God, 'If he will contend with him, he cannot answer him one of a thousand.' Not to one question of a thousand which God can put to him, not for one action of a thousand which himself hath wrought. Alas, is he just, who is so far from ability to justify all he doth, that he cannot justify one act of a thousand that he doth?

Angels are just, they are righteous in their natures, have no spot in their lives, have no error, Ps. 103:20. But are they righteous to God, or before God? No, Job 4:16–18. Angels are nothing in justice to God; though they are just to man, they are unjust to God. They are in a possibility, considered in themselves, of actual injustice, which God is not; he is incapable of being unjust. Again, the law or rule of angels' righteousness is without them, and distinct from them, and thereby they are the more capable of swerving from it; but the law or rule of God's justice is within him, yea, it is himself; he is his own law, his own rule, and therefore it is impossible for him to recede or err from it. When the workman and his rule are different, there may be fear of wandering from his rule; for though the rule be straight, yet the man may, through the mistake of his eye, or shaking of his hand, draw a crooked line; but when the workman and his rule are the same, there is no fear. God's will, that acteth all things, is the rule by which he acteth; and therefore every line must be straight, and every action just. He can never err in anything he doth, whose will is the rule of all he doth, nay, whose actions are their own rule. Such is the creature's weakness that he may wander out of his way; but such is the Creator's power and perfection that he cannot possibly wander, because he is his own way: Dan. 4:35, I Nebuchadnezzar blessed the Most High, who doth according to his will in the army of heaven, and among the inhabitants of the earth.' Observe, who doth according to his will, that is his essential eternal rule. God doth so much surpass men and angels in justice, that he is said to be the habitation of justice: Jer. 1:7, 'They have sinned against the Lord, the habitation of justice,' as if justice dwelt no where, had no abode, but in him and with him.

VIII

GOD INCOMPARABLE IN HIS ATTRIBUTES, IN HIS KNOWLEDGE AND FAITHFULNESS

(5). God is incomparable in his knowledge. Knowledge is that attribute of God, whereby he understandeth all things in and of himself. He is styled in the Scriptures, 1 Sam. 2:3, a God of knowledge: 'The Lord is a God of knowledge, and by him actions are weighed.' As Christ is called a 'Man of sorrows,' Isa. 53:3, to express the greatness of his griefs, to denote him one made up of sorrow, little else than sorrow; so God is called a God of knowledge, to express the greatness of his knowledge, as if he were wholly and only knowledge. Hence he hath eyes and ears attributed to him, because he knoweth all that is done as an eye-witness, and whatsoever is spoken as an ear-witness, 2 Chron. 16:9; Ps. 11:7.

The understanding of God is, like himself, infinite, without bounds or limits: Ps. 147:5, 'His understanding is infinite.' He is said, Job 37:16, to be perfect in knowledge, not only comparatively, as one man may be in respect of another, or as an angel may be in respect of man; but absolutely. To his knowledge nothing can be given or added, from his knowledge nothing can be taken. His knowledge is so perfect that it admits not of an increase or decrease. Men are knowing: Solomon was famous for knowledge, 1 Chron. 1:12; he could speak of the nature of all plants, from the cedar to the hyssop, 1 Kings 4:33. The Romans are said to be filled with all knowledge, Rom. 15:14. Angels are more knowing than men; flesh is dull-sighted, and of dim understanding; spirits have sharper wits, and quicker apprehensions. The devil, though a fallen angel, hath one of his names, Dæmon, from his knowledge. Elect angels surely know much more than devils, for they always behold the face of their Father; and in that face, as in a glass, behold more than human eyes can discern, or evil angels conceive. The spirits of just men in heaven see face to face, and know as they are known, understand very much more than they could here below; but angels, as their understandings are of larger capacity, and their natures more excellent, must needs know more than men. But do men or angels know as God? Can it be said of any man, of any angel, he is perfect in knowledge? His knowledge is incapable of addition or diminution? Can it be said of any man, any angel, his knowledge is infinite? Man's knowledge in this world is little in comparison of what it shall be, yea, nothing. 'We are but of yesterday, and know nothing,' Job 8:3. He is but of small continuance here, and hath but little experience, and therefore must have but little knowledge, yea, so little that it is called nothing; yea, the knowledge of men and angels in the other world will be so little, though enough for their perfection and satisfaction, that it will be nothing in comparison of the knowledge of God; finite knowledge is nothing compared with that knowledge which is infinite.

Whether you consider the matter or object of God's knowledge, or the manner or way of it, he is incomparable in it.

i. If you consider the matter or object of his knowledge: God knoweth all things: John 21:17, 'Lord, thou knowest all things:' 1 John 3:20, 'God is greater than our hearts, for he knoweth all things.' He knoweth whatsoever hath been, whatsoever is, whatsoever shall be, whatsoever can be, whatsoever cannot be. He knoweth all substances, accidents, necessary, contingent things. He makes all, upholds all, governs all, and discerneth all. 'The eyes of the Lord are in every place,' 2 Chron. 16:9.

He knoweth those things that are most hidden, most secret, the hearts, the thoughts, the most close retired motions of the spirit of man: 1 Cor. 2:11, 'What man knoweth the things of a man, but the spirit of a man that is in him?' Yea, what angel knoweth the things of a man? But God doth: 'Hell and destruction are before the Lord: how much more the hearts of the children of men?' Prov. 15:11. Hell seems to be far from his sight, and very remote from heaven his seat. The hearts of the children of men seem to be unsearchable, so deep that none can fathom them; but he hath a line that will sound these depths. He knoweth the spirit of man better than man knoweth himself: 'The heart is deceitful, and desperately wicked: who knoweth it? (No man, no angel knoweth it.) 'I the Lord search the heart,' Jer. 17:9, 10. And none knoweth it but he, therefore he is incomparable herein: 'For thou, thou only, knowest the hearts of the children of men,' 1 Kings 8:39. It is his sole prerogative. Men and angels may see the skins and colours, and lineaments and proportions, and faces and garments, or outsides of things; but God seeth the insides, he pryeth into the very bowels of things, 1 Sam. 16:7. All things are naked and dissected and anatomised before him, Heb. 4:13; 1 Chron. 28:9; Ps. 7:10; Jer. 11:20.

He knoweth what is future, as well as what is past and present: 'Thou knowest my thoughts afar off,' Ps. 139:2. Long before I think them; they are in thy thoughts, before they are in my heart. Man knoweth not what a day is big with, or may bring forth, Prov. 27:1, nor angels neither; but God knoweth what is in the womb of eternity, what all ages and generations shall produce: 'He declares the end from the beginning, and from ancient time the things that are not yet done,' Isa. 46:10. And tells us this is proper to himself: 'Let them declare the things that shall come to pass, that we may know that they are gods,' Isa. 41:23. Let them foretell what is future, and we will believe their deity. Predictions are *arcana imperii*,[16] those secret things that belong only to God, Deut. 29:29; Isa. 41:22, 23, 26.

ii. He is incomparable in the manner of his knowledge. God knoweth all things fully and perfectly; men and angels know, what they do know, but imperfectly and by halves. They know but part of what is knowable, and they know this but in part. God beholds everything thoroughly, as if, like a well-drawn picture, he beheld that alone, and none but that, 2 Chron. 16:9; his eyelids try the children of men, Ps. 11:5, i.e., he hath a distinct, certain, critical, thorough knowledge of them.

God knoweth all things immediately, by immediate intuition, not by species. Men know things either by the senses, the eyes, ears, or tastes; or by species taken in by the sense, and imprinted on the fantasy, which are thence offered to the understanding; or else by faith, and the report of others, or by discourse and ratiocination. He knoweth one thing by another, the conclusion by mediums and premises; the causes by the effects, and the consequents by the antecedents. Saints and angels in heaven know things in God, not in themselves. God knoweth all things in themselves, and seeth all things in himself, as in a glass. Man in this world must have a twofold light to see by; a light in his eye, and a light in the air. But the Father of lights needs no light to see by: 'Darkness and light are both alike to him,' Ps. 139:12; his eyes are as a flame of fire, he seeth in the dark, Rev. 1:14.

God knoweth all things at once, *uno actu et uno ictu*,[17] as they say. Creatures know one thing by another, and one thing after another; their understandings are unable to take in many objects at once, much less able to take in all objects at once; but God seeth all things at one view: 'The Lord looketh

---

[16] "The secret things of the supreme power."
[17] "By one act and one stoke."

down from heaven; he beholdeth all the children of men. From the place of his habitation he beholdeth all the inhabitants of the earth,' Ps. 33:13, 14. The eye of man may see many things at once, as a hive of bees, but if it will see other things, it must remove the sight; though the mind of man can take in more than the eye, as a whole country or world at once, yet it is only the lump or gross. If it would take the distinct knowledge of them, it must remove from thought to thought; but God takes all distinctly, particularly, at once.

God knoweth all things from everlasting, before ever the world had a being. Men and angels may know what is, when it is, but cannot know it as God doth, before it was: Acts 15:18, 'Known to God are all his works, from the beginning of the world.' Before he erected the curious frame of the world, he knew all the rooms and furniture in it, all the motions and actions of all the inhabitants of it. He doth by one pure, simple, undivided, eternal act of his understanding, know all things perfectly, immediately, distinctly, every moment.

(6). God is incomparable in his truth and faithfulness. Truth is that attribute in God whereby he is in himself, as he reveals himself to be, and in his sayings and doings, as he speaketh and acteth.

God is truth in himself, and truth towards his creatures. He is truth in himself:—1. As he truly is, and really existeth. Hence he is styled the true God, Jer. 10:10; John 17:3, in opposition to idols, or false gods, 1 Thes. 1:9. So he is truly infinite, truly all-sufficient, truly eternal, truly immutable, &c. 2. As he is the unchangeable archetype and idea of all true things without himself, so all created things are true, as they answer their patterns in his mind. 3. In his immanent actions, as his decrees and eternal resolutions are all certain, and attain a punctual accomplishment, Ps. 33:11. He is never deceived nor disappointed in his purposes.

God is truth towards his creatures: i. In his works, as all his actions of creation, preservation, government, redemption, are real; and not chimeras or appearances, Rev. 15:3; Ps. 111:7; Deut. 32:4; Ps. 25:10.

ii. In his words: all he saith is truth; his precepts are true, a perfect rule of holiness, without any defect: Ps. 119:86, 'All thy commandments are faithfulness;' ver. 142, 'Thy law is the truth.' All his promises are true, and shall be performed: 'Not one good thing faileth of all that the Lord our God hath promised,' Josh. 23:14. Hence the gospel, the compendium of all the promises, is often called the word of truth, James 1:18. And the covenant of grace is called sure mercies, Isa. 55:3. All his predictions are true, and come to pass in their season, Hab. 2:3; Rev. 22:6, 7. 'These are true and faithful sayings,' Gen. 49:10.

His threatenings are true, and fail not of their accomplishment, 2 Kings 9:26, 36; Rom. 2:2.

He is truth itself, John 14:6, and 17:6; abundant in truth, Exod. 34:6; truth, truth; the Lord God of truth, Ps. 31:5; a God that cannot lie, Titus 1:2. All lying ariseth either from forgetfulness; men break their word, because their memories are slippery; but *oblivio non cadit in Deum,*[18] he is ever mindful of his word, Luke 1:72. To remember his holy covenant, Ps. 106:46, and 111:5, He will ever be mindful of his covenant. Or from weakness, some would, but want power to make good their promises; though they were able when they promised, yet they are by some providence or other disabled, before the day of performance comes; but the strength of Israel cannot lie, 1 Sam. 15:29. The rock, the eternity of Israel cannot lie. Or from wickedness, some can but will not make good their words; but God cannot be charged with any wickedness: Ps. 92:15, 'There is no unrighteousness in him,' 1 Kings 22:23; Ezek. 14:9.

Men may be true, Ps. 15:4; angels are true; but neither men nor angels are true as God is, let them be put in the scales with God; 'And men of high degree are vanity, and angels of the highest degree are a lie: to be laid in the balance, they are altogether lighter than vanity,' Ps. 62:9. Read over God's truth in himself, and you will see how far angels come short thereof. Are they the exemplar of all things? Are all things true as they agree with the ideas in their minds? Consider his truth towards his creatures. Can it be said of an angel as of God, 'The angel that cannot lie hath promised'? Titus 1:2. Are they under an absolute impossibility of deceiving? Surely if they be considered in themselves, it was as possible for them to lie as for the father of lies. It is said of God, 'It is impossible for him to lie,' Heb. 6:18. But this cannot be spoken of elect angels considered in themselves. God is so true that he only is true, all to him are liars, Rom. 3:4; Rev. 3:7, 14.

---

[18] "Forgetfulness does not occur in God."

IX

GOD INCOMPARABLE IN HIS MERCY AND PATIENCE

(7). God is incomparable in his mercy. Mercy is an attribute of God, whereby he pitieth and relieveth his creature in misery. It is an attribute which relateth to the creature only; God knoweth himself, and loveth himself, and glorifieth himself; but he is not merciful to himself. It is an attribute that relateth to the creature in misery. Justice seeks a worthy object, grace is exercised towards an unworthy object, but mercy looks out for a needy, an indigent object. God is bountiful and gracious to elect angels, because they could not deserve that perfection and happiness which they enjoy; but he is not merciful to them, for they were never miserable. Fallen man is the proper object of mercy, as being not only undeserving of the least good, but as also having plunged himself into all evil. Mercy is an attribute, whereby he pitieth his creature in misery; hence he is said in Scripture, after the manner of men, to have tender mercies, Ps. 25:6; and bowels of mercy, Luke 1:58; and to be afflicted in the afflictions of his people, Isa. 63:9; and to have his soul grieved for the miseries of Israel, Judges 10:15, 16. As tender parents are extremely troubled for the afflictions of their children, Ps. 103:12, 13, so his bowels are turned within him, his repentings are kindled together, Hosea 11:8, 9. Mercy doth not only pity, but also relieve the afflicted; it hath a hand to supply, as well as a heart to pity those that are in distress, Isa. 34:17; Gen. 19:16.

The attribute of mercy is that which God glorieth in, and boasteth of, Exod. 33:19; Ps. 103:8. Noble and heroic spirits are ever gentle and merciful; the basest minds are most cruel, and farthest from mercy. God saith, Fury is not in him,' Isa. 27:4; 'judgment is his strange work,' Isa. 28:21; He doth not afflict willingly,' Lam. 3:33; but 'delighteth in the prosperity of his servants,' Ps. 35:27. It is not his nature to disturb and destroy men, it is their sin that forceth thunderbolts into his hands, Isa. 44:22; his delight is in mercy,

Micah 7:18. The blessed God hath multitude of mercies, Ps. 51:1, to answer the multitude of the creature's miseries, abundant mercy, 1 Pet. 1:3. He is said to be rich in mercy, Eph. 2:4. 'Exceeding abundant rich in mercy,' Eph. 2:7. His mercy, as oil, swims on the top of all his attributes, is his delight: Jer. 32:41, 'I will rejoice over them, to do them good.' His mercy, as gold, being most excellent, overlayeth all his works: Ps. 145:7, 'His tender mercy is over all his works.' His mercy is to all admiration: 'Oh how excellent is thy lovingkindness,' Ps. 36:7. 'Oh how great is thy goodness,' Ps. 31:19. His mercy is beyond all apprehension; 'Thy mercy reacheth to the heavens,' Ps. 108:4; 1 Cor. 2:9. He is styled the Father of mercies, 1 Cor. 1:3; not the Father of justice or fury.

Mercy is the joy and pleasure of God; hence he is said to have a mercys-eat, and to have a throne of grace, Heb. 9:5. Sitting is a posture of ease and rest, but he riseth to execute justice, Ps. 68:1. He doth rest in his love, Zeph. 3:17. Mercy is the glory and honour of God. When Moses desired to see the glory of God, Exod. 33:18, the Lord proclaims, 'The Lord God gracious, merciful,' Exod. 34:6, 7. When God promiseth to do great things for his people, that he will give them health, abundance of peace, cleanse them from all their filthiness, and pardon all their iniquities, Jer. 33:7–9; he gives us the fruit of it: ver. 9, 'And it shall be to me for a name of joy, a praise and glory before all nations.' His mercy is his riches, his treasure; hence he is said to be rich in mercy, Eph. 2:4.

God is merciful in all he doth, universally merciful: 'All his ways are mercy and truth,' Ps. 25:10. The whole world is a volume written within and without with characters of mercy. He is merciful to all men, Ps. 145:9; Sheweth mercy to thousands, Exod. 20:6 and 34:7; Mat. 5:45, 46. He is merciful at all times; 'His mercy endureth forever,' Ps. 118:1, and 136:1–3. He is merciful in all respects; he giveth all sorts of mercies, 1 Tim. 6:13; Eph. 1:3; 2 Pet. 1:3, 4.

Men are merciful, Prov. 11:17; Ps. 37:26; so are angels in a sense; but none of them comparable to God. The tender mercies of the wicked, yea, of the righteous men, yea, of angels, are cruelties to the mercies of God. Have they such pity, such bowels for miserable creatures, as God hath?

Have they such power, such ability, to relieve afflicted ones, as God hath? Can they afford preserving, protecting mercy as God, Job 10:12; pardoning and forgiving mercy, Micah 7:18; purifying and renewing mercy, Eph. 2:4; saving and eternal mercy? Titus 3:5, 6. Oh how infinitely short do they come of him! He is so incomparable in mercy, that mercy is said to belong only to him: 'Unto thee, O Lord, belongeth mercy,' Ps. 62:10; unto thee, and none but thee. He is so merciful, that when his bowels conflict with justice on the behalf of sinners, and get the upper hand, he rejoiceth in the victory; 'Mercy rejoiceth against judgment,' James 2:14. He is so merciful, that he dispenseth with his own institutions for the sake of it, Hosea 6:6; Mat. 9:13, with 12:7. Once more, he is so merciful, that he is upbraided with it, as if he were too fond of that attribute, and loved it overmuch: Jonah 4:2, 'Was not this my saying in my own country? For I knew that thou wast merciful.' Thou didst send me to preach destruction and desolation to Nineveh, but when I received the message, I knew all would be prevented by mercy, and that to preach such a threatening was but to disgrace and dishonour myself, as a false prophet, before the men of Nineveh; for I thought then what is now come to pass, that, notwithstanding the peremptoriness of the message, mercy would interpose, and prove me false.

(8). God is incomparable in his patience. Patience is that attribute in God whereby he beareth with sinners, and forbears or defers their punishment, or that whereby he expecteth and waiteth long for their conversion. He is a God slow to anger, Ps. 103:8. He waiteth on men to do them good, Isa. 30:18. He is long-suffering, 2 Pet. 3:7, 9. Nay, he endureth with much long-suffering the vessels of wrath, Rom. 9:22. He is the God of patience, Rom. 15:5.

The patience of God is the more admirable if we consider—

i. How perfectly he hateth sin, Ps. 5:4; Hab. 1:13; Prov. 6:16. And how offensive it is to him, it grieveth him, Eph. 4:30. It presseth him as sheaves press a cart, Amos 2:13. He is broken with their whorish hearts, Ezek. 6:9. Though he be so infinitely perfect that no sin can be hurtful to him, yet he is so infinitely pure that all sin is hateful to him.

ii. What an affront sin is to him, a contempt of his authority, therefore called a despising him, 1 Sam. 2:30. An eclipsing his honour, therefore called a dishonouring him, Rom. 2:23. A contention with him for mastery, therefore called a fighting against him, Acts 5:39; Job 15:25. A violation of his commands, therefore called a transgression of the law, 1 John 3:4. It affronts his wisdom, therefore called folly, 2 Sam. 24:10; his justice, therefore called unrighteousness, 1 John 1:6, 7; his patience, therefore called a despising his long-suffering, Rom. 2:4; his mercy, therefore called a turning his grace into wantonness, Jude 4; his truth, therefore called a lie, Isa. 44:20. It must be infinite patience to bear with that which is the object of infinite hatred.

iii. Who they are who thus dare and provoke him? They are his creatures, Ps. 100:2, whom he hath infinitely obliged, Lam. 3:22, 23; and laden
with innumerable blessings, Ps. 116:12; and loved inconceivably, John 3:16;
and seeks daily to overcome with his kindness, Ps. 130:5; Hosea 11:1. Yet
these turn rebels and traitors, devise and endeavour his ruin, and join with
Satan, his arch-enemy, in order thereunto, Eph. 2:2, 3; Job 15:25, 26.

iv. That he knoweth all men's sins, the number of them, the nature of
them, all the aggravations they admit of. He knoweth their thoughts,
words, actions, Ps. 139. 'I know all their wickedness and all their sins,' Amos
5:12; Ezek. 11:5.

v. That he hath power in his hands to avenge himself when he pleaseth.
He can look, speak, think his creature into hell-fire. Here is the miracle: 'He
that is great in power is slow to anger,' Nah. 1:3.

vi. That he is the more provoked because of his patience. The revenues
of heaven are at present impaired by it. Good men hereby question and
quarrel with his providence, Ps. 73:2–4; Jer. 12:1–3. Bad men hereby are en-
couraged to continue in sin, and to judge him an abettor of their profaneness, Eccles. 8:11; Ps. 50:21.

vii. That he beareth, notwithstanding all this, year after year, many
years; forty years with the Jews, Ps. 95:10; with the whole world one hundred and twenty years, Gen. 6:3; with the Amorites four hundred years, Gen.
15:13, 14.

viii. That he doth not only forbear them, but also do them good. He continueth life, and health, and food, and raiment, and friends, and relations;
nay, the gospel and salvation, and seasons of grace, and tenders of his love
and favour, and of everlasting life, Acts 17:17, 18, 27, 28; Luke 19:41; Job
21:14–16; 2 Cor. 5:19, 20.

Men are patient. Moses was the meekest man on earth, Num. 12:12; but
could he bear as God? No. When the Israelites provoked him, he was impatient: Ps. 106:33, 'They provoked his spirit, that he spake unadvisedly with
his lips.' The apostles were good men; yet, upon a little affront, they call for
fire from heaven, Luke 9:54. If God should be as impatient towards the most
patient men as they are towards others, woe would be to them that ever
they were born.

But though men come short, yet are not angels as patient as God? Surely
no. Angels cannot bear like God with such a froward, peevish piece as man
is. The Lord told Moses that 'he would not go up in the midst of them, lest
he should consume them for their sins; but he would send an angel before
them, to drive out the Canaanites,' Exod. 33:2. Yet, ver. 4, 'When the people

heard these evil tidings, they mourned; and no man did put on his orna-ments.' What evil tidings? 1. They should have an angel for their guide and guard, that was both stronger and wiser than any man. 2. An angel that 'should drive out their enemies,' (God undertaketh for that,) and bring them into the best country under heaven. 3. God gives them the reason why he declines their immediate conduct, lest their stubbornness should pro-voke him to destroy them; yet they weep and mourn at these tidings. Alas! they knew if God could not bear with their provocations, much less could angels; and therefore, if angels be their guides, they must perish. If they could tire out infinite forbearance, and drain an ocean, they must needs quickly tire out finite patience, and drain a little stream. How soon would limited forbearance and a drop of patience be spent! God is so incompara-ble in his patience that he is called 'the God of all patience;' not only be-cause he hath all manner of patience in him, but because he hath engrossed it all to himself.

X

GOD INCOMPARABLE IN HIS ATTRIBUTES, AS THEY ARE FROM HIM, AS THEY ARE HIS ESSENCE, AS THEY ARE ALL ONE IN HIM, AS THEY ARE IN HIM IN AN INFINITE MANNER

2. I shall shew more specially the difference between God and his creatures in reference to these communicable attributes.

(1). These attributes are all essential to God. They are from God, as well as in God. He is their author as well as their subject. But in men and angels they are all derivative: though truth and justice and holiness may be in them, yet they are not from them, but from God. God is not obliged to any but himself for them, he can thank only himself that he hath them; but angels and men are not obliged to themselves, but to him for them. When the high God would lay Job low, by manifesting the vast difference between himself and Job, he bids Job be obliged to himself for his excellency: Job 40:10, 'Deck thyself with majesty and excellency; array thyself with glory and beauty.' To be decked and arrayed with majesty and excellency, notes, 1. The extent and abundance of it—the whole man is covered with raiment. To be clothed with shame, is to be extremely reproached, Ps. 35:26. To be arrayed with humility, is to be very humble, lowly in an extraordinary degree, 1 Pet. 5:5. 2. The publicness of it. Our deckings and raiments are visible; we cannot go abroad but all see our clothes. God speaks to Job to this purpose: Job, thou hast talked very presumptuously, and carried thyself as if there were no great distance or difference between me and thyself, as if thou wert like me, and equal to me. If thou art, let me see it; deck thyself with majesty and excellency, array thyself with glory and beauty. I can deck myself, and array myself with all these in the highest degree, and will not be beholden to any others for their help; I am clothed with majesty, but no creature lent a hand for the making up or putting on those clothes; Ps. 104:1. 'I have covered myself with light as with a garment,' Ps. 104:2. But neither man nor angel afforded me the least assistance therein. Do thou as much for thyself as I have done for myself, and then indeed thou mayest compare with me. God might make the same offer to angels which he doth to Job, and none of them would or could accept it. Dependence is of their essence, as they are creatures; and they can no more be separated from it than from themselves.

(2). These attributes are the very essence of God, not qualities or properties, as in men and angels. The holiness of God is the holy God; 'Once have I sworn by my holiness,' Ps. 89:36; i.e., by myself, 'that I will not lie unto David;' for Heb. 6:13, 'God having no greater to swear by, swore by himself.' The power of God is the powerful God, the truth of God is the true God, the wisdom of God is the wise God. All his attributes are himself, his essence; in men and angels, their wisdom, and power, and justice, and truth, are accidents, and differ from their substances; and this is apparent, because angels and men may be, and are, without these attributes, as devils and wicked men. In them these properties are one thing and their essence is another thing, so that they may be separated. An angel may be an angel, and not holy, nor wise, nor just, &c. A man may be a man, and not powerful, nor patient, nor merciful; and the reason is, because these properties are really distinct from the essences of men or angels; but in God they are his very being and essence; they are himself, and can no way be separated from him, no more than he can be separated from himself: God could not be God if he were not most wise, most holy, most just, most patient, &c. God's attributes are one most pure essence diversely apprehended of us, as it is diversely manifested to us. God's punishing the wicked is his justice; God's performing his promises is his faithfulness; his relieving the miserable is his mercy; his bearing with the guilty is his patience; so are all his essence, himself.

(3). Those attributes are all one in God. His justice is his mercy, and his wisdom is his patience, and his knowledge is his faithfulness, and his mercy is his justice, &c. Though they are distinguished in regard of their objects, and in regard of our apprehensions of them, and in regard of their effects, yet they are all one in themselves; and this floweth from the former head, because they are the essence of God, and his essence is a pure undivided being. In men and angels, these attributes or perfections are different and several, for they may have one without the other. Their righteousness is one thing, and their power another thing, and their truth a third thing; for we see in angels some that are strong and powerful that are not righteous or faithful, and among men some have one of these perfections who have not another; yea, though in good men all these perfections are in some degree, yet all are not in any one in the same degree. There is scarce any saint who is not more eminent for some spiritual excellency than for others; but in God they are all one and the same; as when the sunbeams shine through a yellow glass they are yellow, a green glass they are green, a red glass they are red, and yet all the while the beams are the same; or as, when the sun shines on clay it hardens it, on wax it softens it, on sweet flowers it draweth out their fragrancy, on dunghills and ditches it draweth out their ill savours, yet still it is the same sun and the same influences; the difference lieth in the objects and the effects. So the great God, who is always working in the world, when he worketh towards the wicked in punishing he is righteous, towards the godly in saving them he is merciful; yet still the same immutable God.

(4). All these attributes are in God in the highest degree, yea, beyond all degrees. These communicable attributes which are in angels and men in degrees, and limited, for a finite substance will not admit of an infinite property, are in God infinitely. Immensity, like a golden thread, runs through all his communicable properties: his understanding is infinite, Ps. 147:5. So his justice is infinite, his mercy is infinite, and all the rest. They have no bounds, no limits, but his own will and pleasure. He never acted to the utmost in any of them; he never put forth so much power, but he could put forth more if he pleased; he never exercised so much patience, but he could exercise more if he would.

Hence it is that in Scripture they are affirmed of God not only in the concrete, but also in the abstract. He is not only loving, but love: 'God is love,' 1 John 4:7. He is not only wise, but wisdom: Prov. 9:1, 'Wisdom hath built her house.' He is not only good, but goodness: 'I will make all my goodness,' i.e., myself, 'pass before thee,' Exod. 33:19. He is not only holy, but holiness: 'Look down from heaven, the habitation where thy holiness dwelleth,' Isa. 63:15. Therefore these attributes of God must be boundless, because they are his being, himself.

XI

GOD INCOMPARABLE IN HIS WORKS, CREATION, AND PROVIDENCE

Thirdly, God is incomparable in his works, as well as in his being and attributes: none hath such a strong hand, such a stretched out arm, or can do like him. 'O Lord,' saith Moses, 'thou hast begun to shew to thy servant thy greatness, and thy mighty hand: for what God is there in heaven or on earth, that can do according to thy works?' Deut. 3:24. He is a God doing wonders, Exod. 15:11. His doings are like his being: he works like a God: Isa. 28:29, 'He is wonderful in counsel, and excellent in working.' His works are all wonderful: Ps. 86:10, 'Thou dost marvellous things, thou art God alone.' He doth *miranda stupenda*,[19] so that it is said of him, Num. 23:23, 'What hath God wrought?' His works are great, Joel 2:21; 'honourable and glorious,' Ps. 111:3; 'perfect,' Deut. 32:4. 'God thundereth marvellously with his voice; great things doeth he, which we cannot comprehend,' Job 37:5. The works of men and angels are little, small; some mean things they do by divine concurrence; but his works are great and unsearchable, which we cannot comprehend. If creatures do great things, in a sense, or comparatively, yet they may be found out; their fellow-creatures have a clue which will lead them into all their labyrinths, and a line which will sound the bottom of all their actions; but God's works cannot be comprehended by the understandings of any creature: 'O the depth of the wisdom and knowledge of God; how unsearchable are his ways, and doings past finding out,' Rom. 11:33; 'His footsteps are not known,' Ps. 77:19; yea, 'He doth great things, and unsearchable, and marvellous things without number,' Job 5:9, till there be no number. If creatures do great things, and marvellous and unsearchable; yet you might soon reckon up all such works of theirs, one great, marvellous, unsearchable thing were enough for the whole creation;

---

[19] "Marvelous things, stupendous things."

but God doth great things and unsearchable, yea, marvellous things without number. His ways are not as man's ways: 'As far as the heavens are higher than the earth, so far are his ways above the ways of man,' Isa. 55:8, 9. No ways like his; among all the gods, there is none like unto him; neither are there any works like unto his works, Ps. 86:8. Whether you consider the matter of his works, and the works themselves, or his manner of working.

1. His works themselves, and therein I shall pass by his internal works, both personal and effectual, and mention only his external works.

He is incomparable in what works he is pleased to do, or hath done.

(1). Creation, herein he is incomparable: *creatura non potest creare*, the creature cannot create; *ex nihilo nihil fit*[20] with them: man may do something towards the emendation of the form, but he cannot produce matter, no, nor mend it when it is before him. A goldsmith may make a sparkling jewel, but then you must give him gold and precious stones to make it of; he can put the matter into a better form, but he is so far from making matter where there is none, that he cannot mend the matter which you give him: he cannot make gold of silver, nor diamonds of common stones. Man's work may exceed the matter, but man's work cannot make the matter exceed itself. But God can not only make the matter to exceed itself,—as in man, who is formed of the dust of the earth, he hath such curious parts, veins, sinews, arteries, &c.; such members, eyes, cheeks, ears, &c.; such characters of beauty on the whole, that he looks nothing like his parent earth, the matter of which he was made,— but also make matter: he hath brought something, nay, all things out of nothing. All the angels and men cannot create one grain of corn, one pile of grass, one mote of dust; but the great God hath erected the stately fabric of heaven and the earth, with the curious steps and stories thereof, and the various creatures and furniture therein, of nothing. Hereby he proves himself the true God, 'The living God that made heaven and earth, and all things therein,' Acts 14:15. He proves his deity hereby, Jer. 10:10– 12, 'The gods that have not made the heavens and the earth, shall perish from the earth, and from under the heavens. He hath made the earth by his power, he hath established the world by his wisdom, and stretched out the heavens by his discretion;' i.e. can you be so foolish and sottish, as to imagine that blind, dumb, deaf, dead idols can compare with him who created you and all things beside? When God would proclaim his sovereignty and incomparable excellency, he challengeth Job, 'Where wast thou when I laid the foundations of the earth? Declare, if thou

---

[20] "From nothing, nothing comes."

hast understanding. Who hath laid the measures thereof, or stretched the line upon it? Whereupon are the foundations thereof set? Or who laid the corner-stone thereof?' Job 38:4, 5. God would here denote the exactness and accurateness of his works, and so he alludes to men, who, when they would set up a strong, stately, neat, compact dwelling, lay the foundations and corner-stones, and all the rest, by line and measure. But that which God would principally intimate here, is his own omnipotency, and man's impotency: 'Where wast thou when I laid the foundations of the earth?' &c. Didst thou then lend me a helping head how to do it, or a helping hand in the doing of it? Surely no, I did all myself. Those innumerable beings which are on earth, and in the ocean, yea, that are included within the vast circumference of the highest heavens, are all made by him out of nothing: 'Through faith we believe that the worlds were made by the word of God, so that things which are seen were not made of things that do appear,' Heb. 11:3. The great God had no materials to make the great house with, he did not frame it of his own essence, or any pre-existent matter, Isa. 45:12. Yet such admirable qualities are everywhere intermixed, matter and form, subject and accidents, power and goodness, wisdom and order; a rare symmetry, exact proportion, and beauty on the whole; a dependent subordination, and useful subserviency in every part, so equally poised, that it is hard to determine which bears the greatest weight in the mighty work, and gives abundant cause to cry out with the psalmist, 'O Lord, how marvellous are thy works! in wisdom hast thou made them all,' Ps. 104:24.

(2). He is incomparable in regard of providence: i. For preservation none is like him, nay, none beside him doth this; 'O thou preserver of men;' Job 7:20; 'thy visitation preserveth my spirit,' Job 10:12. God is unlike to men; the carpenters or masons build houses, and then leave them to the care and charge of others; but God keeps up what he sets up. His providence succeedeth creation, and is indeed a continual creation: 'Thou preservest man and beast,' Ps. 36:6. Not food, or air, or sleep, but 'thou preservest man and beast:' and not only men and beasts, but 'all things subsist by him,' Col. 1:17. That hand alone which made all, can maintain all; and that power only which produced out of nothing, must preserve from nothing, Acts 17:28. 'In him we live, and move, and have our beings.' That being which gave us our beings, must uphold us in our beings: Heb. 1:3, 'He upholdeth all things by the word of his power.' 1. *Sustinendo*,[21] as a pillar, or sure foundation, upon

---

[21] "By sustaining."

which they stand. The air which surrounds the earth and ocean, cannot bear a feather, yet in it hangeth the massy weight of earth and sea: Job 26:7, 'He hangeth the earth'—i.e., earth and sea, the terrestrial globe—'upon nothing:' his power is the only pillar that bears them up. 2. *Influendo*,[22] as a fountain from which they derive all their virtue and operations: the beings and motions of all his creatures depend wholly upon his concurrence. If he suspend his influence, *coactum secundum*,[23] according to the schoolmen, the fire will not burn, Dan. 3:27. Neither can the best eyes see, though the faculty be well-disposed, and the object be coloured, and at a good distance, Gen. 19:7, as hath been hinted before. It is natural to the sun to run his race strongly and swiftly, yet if he doth not concur, as swift as the sun is, he cannot creep a snail's pace; he standeth still in Gibeah, Josh. 10:13; Job 9:7. 3. *Constringendo*,[24] as a sovereign bond and ligature, by which the parts of all things hold together, and are kept as water in a vessel, from flowing abroad to their dissolution. No man, no angel, can bear its own weight, much less the weight of another creature: every creature is like a glass without a bottom, which cannot stand alone, but must always be in hand.

It is impossible for the creation, or any part of it, to bear up a moment, if God should forget it, and deny his actual concurrence to it. It doth constantly depend on God, as the figure of the seal imprinted on the water, which being withdrawn, the impression is instantly defaced. God is to the world as the soul to the body, which alone can actuate and move it, without which it cannot stir at all, but is as a dead corpse.

ii. For gubernation; he governeth all, and neither men nor angels can govern themselves. The great family of the world would soon lose its beauty, yea, its being, if he did not maintain its harmony and concord, by guiding them in their motions, keeping them in their several stations, and directing them to their ends: 'The Lord hath established his throne in the heavens, and his kingdom ruleth over all,' Ps. 103:19. One creature would most cruelly devour another; beasts would prey on men: all creatures would become their own enemies and executioners; the whole earth would be turned into an Aceldama, and a Golgotha, a field of blood, and place of skulls, yea, into a hell, if he did not order, and guide, and govern all. Treasons, incest, slaughters, parricides, would overwhelm the whole world, pervert the order of nature, turn all into confusion and destruction, if he

---

[22] "By flowing/influencing."
[23] "According to coaction."
[24] "By restraining."

did not keep the reins in his own hands, and govern all things, in every of their actions, every moment.

He governeth the highest, even the governors themselves on earth, that seem to be above all government: kings and princes seem to be absolute, and wholly at their own disposal; 'Who may say to a king, What dost thou?' Many will tell us that their hands are their own, to do what they please; but more will acknowledge that their hearts are their own, to think as they please. But, alas, they cannot command their hands to do what they will, their hands are ruled and overruled by him, Acts 4:28. 'Herod and Pontius Pilate were gathered together, to do what thy hand determined to be done.' In like manner, their hearts are not in their own hands, to think as they will, but in God's hand, to think what he will: 'The heart of the king is in the hand of the Lord, and he turneth it as the rivers of water, which way he pleaseth,' Prov. 21:1. As the husbandman turneth the sluices into his ground, this way or that way, into this channel or that channel, as he thinks best for his own advantage; so God turneth the hearts of kings this way or that way, which way he seeth most for his glory: Prov. 16:9, 'A man's heart deviseth his way, but the Lord directeth his steps.' No man is master of himself, so much as of his thoughts; that heart that deviseth its way, is directed in those devices by God. The sun is higher than an earthly prince, and seems to be his own guide; he acteth naturally, and so necessarily: 'But if he speak to the sun, it riseth not, and he sealeth up the stars,' Job 9:9. He hath a negative voice upon the motions of all beings.

He governeth the lowest as well as the highest: as none are so high as to be above his precepts, so none are so low as to be below his providence: the highest must remember him, and he doth not forget the lowest: 'Are not two sparrows sold for a farthing, yet not one of them falls to the ground without your Father's providence,' Mat. 10:29. Sparrows seem to fly at liberty, and to fall casually; but even their flight is directed by God, and their fall ordered by him: they neither fly nor fall accidentally, but providentially.

He governeth the most stubborn creatures, those which seem wholly ungovernable. The winds, the high winds, whirlwinds, seem to cast off and scorn all rule and government, but these winds are at his will: 'stormy winds fulfil his word,' Ps. 148:8. When they rush forth with such irresistible force that neither men, nor trees, nor horses can stand before them, he rideth on their wings, and hath them more at command than a skilful rider hath a horse, to turn this way or that way at his pleasure, Ps. 104:3, and 18:10. They are all at his beck: he causeth them to blow, Ps. 147:18, and ceaseth them, Mat. 8:26. The wise man tells us he hath them in his fist, Prov. 30:4. He can hold them fast, or let them loose, as a man what he hath in his fist.

The waves seem rougher than the winds; the waters are moist bodies, that are with much difficulty contained in their own bounds, especially when the winds cross them, and contend with them; but he sitteth on the floods, Ps. 29:11, as a prince on his throne, enjoining and forcing obedience and submission: 'he bindeth the waters in a garment,' Prov. 30:4, as women their sucking infants in mantles, with swaddling-bands, which they cannot get out of; though the sea be such a giant, such a monster, that it swalloweth up thousands, and burieth them in its belly, that it maketh all to shake and tremble when it roareth and rageth, yet to God it is but a little infant, which he ordereth as he pleaseth, and can lay to sleep or make quiet in an instant, when it is never so tempestuous: 'When I made the cloud the garment thereof, and thick darkness its swaddling-band,' Job 38:9. Some earthly princes, heated with passion, and drunk with pride, have cast shackles into the sea, threatening it with bondage if it did not obey them. Xerxes commanded so many strokes to be given the sea, as a punishment of its rebellion against his will; but such actions are the highest folly and madness. Many have had great command at sea, but none ever had the command of the sea save God. As tempestuous and outrageous as it is, it is his quiet prisoner, and stirs not without his leave, nor otherwise than he lengthens its chain: 'I set bars and doors, and said, Hitherto shalt thou come, and no farther, and here shall thy proud waves be stayed,' Job 38:10, 11.

It may easily be proved that the sea is higher than the earth, and why, then, doth it not overflow it, and drown its inhabitants? Surely no reason can be given but the command the great God hath over it: Ps. 104:6–9, 'The waters stood above the mountains; at thy rebuke they fled, at the voice of thy thunder they hasted away: They go up by the mountains, they go down by the valleys, unto the place which thou hast founded for them: Thou hast set a bound, that they may not pass over, that they turn not again to cover the earth.' The waters did once cover the earth, till God broke up for them his decreed place, Job 38:10, and commanded them into their appointed channels. They have a propensity and inclination still to cover the earth again. What doth their constant beating upon their banks with rage and fury, and now and then encroaching upon the earth, and getting ground of it, signify, but their desire and longing to beat down all before them, and turn the dry land into a sea? The only reason why they do not accomplish their ends is, because the great Governor of the world hath set them their bounds, which they cannot pass.

Some men are extreme stubborn and refractory, as immoveable as rocks, resolved and fixed for their own wills and ways; but even these God ordereth at his pleasure. The king of Babylon seemed an untameable beast; he had foraged many countries and kingdoms, and trampled on many idols and false gods; and he cometh in a full career against the people of God, like a lion greedy of his prey, no way doubting but to tear them in pieces and devour them; as you may read in the thirty-seventh and thirty-eighth chapters of Isaiah. But mark how God governs this wild ass, and hath this monster at command: Isa. 37:29, 'I will put my hook into thy nose, and my bridle in thy lips, and I will turn thee back by the way by which thou camest.' I will put my hook into thy nose; an allusion either to a fisher, when he hath the fish fast on his hook, draweth it which way he will, Job 41:1; or to such rings as men put into the noses of bears to keep them in, and govern them with. My bridle into thy lips, Ezek. 19:4, 9, my bit in thy mouth, and my curb about thy jaws; an allusion to them that ride horses, who with bridle and bit rein and restrain them, and keep them within compass, Ps. 32:9; James 3:3. As if God had said, Because thou ravest and ragest like some huge unruly fish, or some fierce wild beast, I will take thee with my hook, and I will ring thee, and curb thee, and lead thee, and draw thee whither I list.

The devils are more untractable than winds, and waves, and men. They have great power, hence called the strong man, Luke 11:21; and powers, Eph. 6:12. Their union doth much increase their strength, *vis unita fortior*.[25] They are so much one in their confederacies, and all their conspiracies, that they are called the evil one, the wicked one, Mat. 13:28; the devil, 1 Pet. 5:8. Because, though they are many thousands, yet they agree and unite against God, as if they were all but one. They have much knowledge, subtility, and policy to direct their power, *vis consilii expers*,[26] &c. Their excellent natures, their great observation of persons and actions, their long experience of some thousands of years in the world, must needs speak their wisdom, or rather craftiness, to be great.

---

[25] "Strength joined is stronger."
[26] "Strength without counsel."

Add to these their innate implacable hatred of God, which makes them employ all their power, and improve all their policy, to offend and displease him, to break from under his yoke and subjection; yet, in spite of all their might, their craft, their malice, he governeth them as a man doth his prisoners whom he hath in fetters: 'He hath reserved them in chains of darkness,' Jude 6. He hath them ever in the chains, 1. Of their own terrifying, affrighting consciences, which allow them no rest day or night. Indeed all time is a dark, dreadful time to them, and all places are dark, dismal places to them. They are, wherever they go, as prisoners with fetters upon them, yea, such shackles as enter into and pierce their spirits; in chains of darkness. 2. In chains of divine providence: God governeth their persons and all their motions; they go no whither but as he pleaseth, though they go up and down in the earth. As subtle a spirit as the devil is, he cannot touch Job, Job 1:12; no, nor the swine, without God's leave, Mat. 8:31. He that would read more of the incomparableness of God in his providence, may see it incomparably set forth by God's own mouth in the 37th, 38th, 39th, 40th, and 41st chapters of Job.

XII

GOD INCOMPARABLE IN THE WORK OF REDEMPTION; HE CAN DO ALL THINGS

(3). He is incomparable in the work of redemption. And truly this work is his masterpiece, pure workmanship; and, indeed, all his works of creation and providence are subordinate to this. All his attributes sparkle most gloriously in this, Ps. 102:16; all his angels in heaven admire and adore him for this, Rev. 4:10, 11. This is the work of all his works, which he is so mightily pleased with, and reapeth so much glory and praise from, Isa. 42:1, and 43:21. No angels, no men, no not all together, could with all their united worthiness redeem one soul: 'None of them can redeem his brother, or give to God a ransom for him. For the redemption of the soul is precious, it ceaseth forever,' Ps. 49:9. 10.

None beside God had pity enough for man's misery, or wisdom enough to find out a remedy, or power enough for his recovery.

None had pity enough for man's misery. Boundless misery called for boundless mercy; one deep for another. But where is such mercy to be found among the creatures? Man was a child of wrath, had plunged himself into an ocean of evils and fury, and this required an ocean of love and pity; but creatures at most had but drops. But the Creator had infinite grace for infinite guilt, and infinite mercy for infinite misery: Ezek. 16:4–6, 'In the day of thy nativity, thou wast cast out, to the loathing of thy person; thy navel was not cut, neither wast thou salted with salt, nor washed with water.' Here is misery indeed, but what help or compassion from creatures? Truly none: no eye pitied thee, to do any of these things unto thee; who then had pity enough? 'Then I passed by thee, and saw thee in thy blood; then was my time of love, and I bid thee live; yea, when thou wast in thy blood, I said unto thee, Live.' God hath great mercy for great misery, Eph. 2:4, 5; abundant mercy for abundant misery, 1 Pet. 1:3; a plaster altogether as broad and as large as the sore, John 3:16; 1 John 4:9; Eph. 3:19; therefore the Holy Ghost observeth, Luke 1:78, in the work of redemption, the tender mercy of our God from on high hath visited us.

None had wisdom enough to find out a remedy. Had the creatures had pity enough, and kindness enough, they had not wisdom enough to make justice and mercy meet together, and righteousness and grace kiss each other. If God should have offered man his pardon and life, upon condition that he with angels should consult, and find out some way to satisfy his infinite justice, that was offended by sin; alas, poor man must of necessity have perished. What creature was able to undertake the satisfaction of infinite justice? It would have bankrupt them all to satisfy for one of the smallest sins. And who could have thought of God the creator to undertake it? Who durst have presumed to entertain such a motion in his heart? Could it have entered into the mind of men or angels, that the law might be fulfilled in its commands and curse, the glory of divine justice and holiness salved, and miserable man eternally saved?

No creature would have thought of a way to reconcile the justice and mercy of God; no creature could have thought of any way for it; nay, no creature durst have thought of such a way as God hath found out. No. He that made the world by his wisdom, Ps. 104:24, when it had unmade itself, new made it by his wisdom. Hence the redemption of man is called τολυποίκιλος σοφία, the manifold, the curious, the embroidered wisdom of God; such wisdom as passed the knowledge of angels, Eph. 3:10; and the Redeemer is called the wisdom of God, 1 Cor. 1:24; in this work is infinite wisdom because in this work infinite justice and infinite mercy do meet, Rom. 3:24, 25; Eph. 2:5, 7; 1 John 4:9, 10.

Again, None had power to have gone through with the work, if they had had wisdom to have found out a way. There was so much to be done in order to man's recovery, that it would have undone all the world, if they had undertaken it. The powers of hell must be overcome, the curse of the law, and wrath of the law-giver, must be borne. Sin, that was so strong and fast in the heart of man, must be subdued; grace and holiness, against which man had an enmity must be infused; and what power less than omnipotent could effect either of these? God, who discovered great power in creating the world of nothing, discovered much greater in redeeming the world when it was worse than nothing. In the former he had no opposition; in the latter his law, justice, the devils of hell, nay, man himself, did resist and oppose him. It had been impossible for the Mediator to have borne up, and held out under all those contests with the powers of darkness, the malediction of the law, the fury of his Father, if the almighty everlasting arms had not been under him. Isa. 42:1, 'Behold my servant, whom I uphold;' Isa. 49:8, 9. Therefore you read of power, great power, mighty power, greatness of power, exceeding greatness of power, put forth in the work of redemption: Eph. 1:19, 20, 'And what is the exceeding greatness of his power to us-ward who believe, according to the working of the mighty power, which he wrought in Christ, when he raised him from the dead;' and the Redeemer is called the power of God, 1 Cor. 1:24; the arm of the Lord, Isa. 53:1; his strength, Isa. 27:5; once more we read, 'Thy redeemer is mighty, the Lord of hosts is his name,' Jer. 50:34.

2. He is incomparable, not only in what he hath done, but also in what he can do. He can do what he will, nay, he can do much more than he will do.

He can do what he will. His arm is as large as his mind, and his hand equal to his heart. His will and pleasure is the only boundary of his strength and power: 'Whatsoever the Lord pleased, that did he in heaven and earth, and the seas, and in all deep places,' Ps. 135:6, and 115:3. Can this be said of men or angels? Can they do what they please? Surely no. But the Lord doth what he hath a mind to do: 'He is of one mind, and who can turn him? And what his soul desireth, that he doth,' Job 23:13. His heart only can limit his hands, and his strength is determined by nothing but his will. It was the saying of a prince, that he could bear a circle about his head, meaning his crown, but he could not bear a circle about his feet, he would go and come at his own pleasure, and do what he thought fit; but all the princes in the world have fetters about their feet, and chains about their hands. They cannot go whither they please; Isa. 37:33, 34, Sennacherib would needs go up to Jerusalem, and bringeth an army against it for that end, but his feet were fettered. 'Thus saith the Lord concerning the king of Assyria, He shall not come into this city; by the way that he came, by the same shall he return.' Neither can they do what they please. As they go, not whither they will, but, whither God pleaseth; so they do, not what they will, but, what God pleaseth, Acts 4:27, 28.

It is God's incomparable prerogative to go whither, and do what he will. God doth not do many things that he can, but he doth all things that he will. He can do more than he will. He cannot do what is sinful, he cannot lie, Titus 1:2; he cannot deny himself, 1 Tim. 2:13. He cannot do that which implieth a contradiction. He cannot make himself a creature, or make a creature a god, because the doing of these things speak weakness and imperfection, but whatsoever speaketh power or perfection, that he can do: 'He is able to do exceeding abundantly above all that we can ask or think,' Eph.

3:20. A man may ask much, this world, the other world, a thousand worlds after them, millions of worlds after those, better worlds, greater worlds, the sovereignty and dominion over them, the command and rule of them for ages, for generations, forever. A man may conceive more than he can ask; the mind of man is much larger than his tongue. His apprehension doth far exceed his expressions, especially of such a man whose mind is enlightened and enlarged, for of such the apostle speaks, and not contracted and narrowed to sublunary sensual objects. But God can do more than we are able to ask or think, yea, abundantly more; so much more, that we cannot think how much more; nay, exceeding abundantly more, ὑπὲρ ἐκ περίσσου, *valde abundanter*, above abundance.

Is anything impossible to God? Luke 1:37. With God all things are possible, Mat. 19:26. He is good at everything that is good. Men are good, some at one thing, some at another thing; so are angels: but no man, no angel is good at all things, God only can do everything, as God only can be everything; he only that is universal in his being is universal in his doings. He can make millions of worlds in a moment, and unmake them again as soon; he can kill and make alive in the twinkling of an eye; he can build up, and pluck down, take nature off its hinges, and set it on again; make the waters, when they run never so violently, to stand still; stop the sun in its full career; keep the hottest fire from burning, or so much as singeing a hair. Shall the sun go backward, saith he, ten degrees, or forward? 2 Kings 20:9, 10; take either, it is all one to me; choose which thou likest best—to me both are equally easy.

XIII

GOD INCOMPARABLE IN THE MANNER OF HIS WORKING: HE WORKETH IRRESISTIBLY, ARBITRARILY

2. If you consider the manner of his working, he is incomparable therein also.

(1). He worketh irresistibly; he worketh so, as none can hinder him: all the united wisdom, power of men, of angels, cannot stop him at his work. The mighty king Nebuchadnezzar was taught this truth, when he was grazing among the beasts: Dan. 4:35, 'He doth according to his will in the armies of heaven, and among the inhabitants of the earth, and none can stay his hand.' Mark, he doth what he will, and none can stay his hand; the prayers of his people have sometimes stayed his hand, when he was going to slay and destroy, but it was because out of his grace he stayed it himself. Alas, what creature can see, or know, or reach his hand, that is invisible and omnipresent? Isa. 46:10,[27] 'My counsel shall stand, and I will do all my pleasure.' The counsels of men do not always stand, he makes them to fail and fall: 'He bringeth the counsels of the heathen to nought, and maketh the devices of the people of none effect,' Ps. 33:10. But none can make his counsel void, or his devices invalid.

What he will do he doth, and there is no withstanding him. If he will bring an enemy against a nation, none can prevent their coming. Calling the ravenous bird from the east, the man that executeth my counsel from a far country—Cyrus that should seize on Babylon, as a ravenous bird on his prey—yea, I have spoken it, and I will bring it to pass. Let me see who shall hinder it; I have purposed it, and I will do it. I would see who dares undertake to oppose it, Isa. 45:11, 12.

If he will deprive men of their honours and grandeur, of their estates and treasures, of their might and power, there is no contending with him,

---

[27] Text: Isa. 48:10.

it must be done: Job 9:12, 'Behold, he taketh away, who can hinder him?' If he will take away, nothing shall stand in his way. The four great strong monarchies of the world, that successively were the dread and terror of the earth, were taken away by him, and who hindered him? All their policy and power could not prevent him, or hinder their ruin, Dan. 2:44.

God hath a negative voice upon the motions of all the creatures: 'Who is he that saith, and it cometh to pass, if the Lord commandeth it not?' Lam. 3:27. They who reckon without him must reckon again; they must ask his leave, as well as have his assistance, or sit still and do nothing. Their wheels, though never so well oiled, stand still, or go backward, if he say nay to their motion forward: 'He speaketh to the sun, and it riseth not; and sealeth up the stars,' Job 9:7. No day, not the least light in the heavens at night, without his leave; but no creature hath a negative voice upon the least of his actions; what he will do he doth, and never asketh men or angels' leave. Nay, challengeth them to hinder him if they can: Isa. 43:13, 'I will work; who shall let it?' Observe his resolution, 'I will work;' he speaks like one in authority, that is above all checks and controls, that can make good what he purposeth in spite of all opposition; I will work. Observe also his challenge, 'Who shall let it?' Would I could see the man, the angel, that durst stand in the way of my motions. The Jews might think Babylon will let; I, saith God, have sent to Babylon, and destroyed all their princes, I have broken in pieces those iron bars; there is no fear that they should hinder my entrance into their city.

He can give a supersedeas to the highest attempts and strongest designs of creatures; he can blow on them, and they are soon blasted, all their politic conceptions prove abortive: 'Take counsel together, and it shall come to nought,' Isa. 8:10. Their most powerful engines prove ineffectual: ver. 9, 'Gird yourselves, and ye shall be broken in pieces.' some of them talked at a great, at a high rate; 'We will go up against Judah and destroy it, and set a king in the midst thereof, even the son of Tabeal;' but they speak beyond their strength, and reckon, as we say, without their host: Thus saith the Lord God, It shall not stand, neither shall it come to pass,' Isa. 7:6, 7. But none can give a supersedeas to the least of his attempts: 'Behold he breaketh down, and it cannot be built up again; he shutteth up a man, and there can be no opening,' Job 12:14.

(2). He worketh arbitrarily, according to his own will; he doth what he will, and he alone may do what he will. It is argued by many, that some princes are not accountable for what they do to any man, but all hold they are accountable to God. They are his stewards and deputies, and must give an account to him of their stewardships. They are his creatures, and are, or ought to be, limited by his laws, and so must be responsible to him for their carriages and government. No king is absolute or arbitrary in his governments, because all kings are his subjects, and owe allegiance to his majesty, and obedience to his commands; but God is absolute and arbitrary, and may do what he will do; everything that he doth is just, because he doth it: 'He doth what he will in heaven and earth, and none can say unto him, What dost thou?' Dan. 4:35. He is responsible to none for any of his actions; none may question him, much less quarrel with him for what he doth. Angels are far from being arbitrary, his will, not their own, is their rule: Ps. 103:20, 'Ye ministers of his that do his pleasure.' He only that is above all law is above all transgression, 1 John 3:4; and he whose will is the only rule, of rectitude and righteousness, may well do what he will, Rom. 12:2.

He hath an absolute illimited propriety in all the works of his hands; he is the great proprietor of all the world, and therefore may dispose of all at his pleasure, Ps. 24:1: Mat. 20:13, 15, 'May I not do what I will with mine own? Friend, I do thee no wrong.' Though men may have a civil right to their estates, and a natural right to themselves and their children, yet the original in all is still God's. He divests himself of nothing by lending anything to us, or trusting us with it; and therefore he may use what is his own, at his own liberty and pleasure, and none may question or quarrel with him for it.

Again, he is supreme, and so above all answering or accounting for anything he doth: he is the most High, Ps. 92:1. It is no disparagement to men or angels to be under a law; nay, it is essential to them as they are creatures; but he that is supreme, and giveth all laws to others, is under no law himself; indeed, if he had a superior, he might be called to account by him: 'But why strivest thou against him? He giveth no account of any of his matters,' Job 33:13. Why strivest thou against him? Not by open force, but secret murmurings, and logical arguings, against his providential dispensations. It is vain, for he giveth no account of any of his matters. He is not bound to tell thee what he doth, or why he doth it. He hath received nothing from thee, and so not bound to account to thee, Rom. 11:35. Thou hast no authority to call him to account; what man or angel hath power to call him to account? In the next chapter the Holy Ghost doth fully speak for our purpose: Job 34:10, 12, 13, 'Far be it from God, that he should do wickedly; and from the Almighty, that he should pervert judgment. Who hath given him a charge of the earth?' Whose deputy is he in the government of the world? If he be a deputy or viceroy to any superior power, then he must keep close to the instructions, and act according to the commission he receiveth from them, or be accountable for his wanderings and deviations; 'But who hath given him a charge over the earth?' What man? What angel? Where is he? What or who is he that hath given him a charge? If there were one higher than God to give him a rule, then if he swerved from it, he was faulty; but because he is higher than the highest of beings, and his own law, therefore he may do what he will without blame: 'Who hath enjoined him his way? Or can say unto God, Thou hast wrought iniquity?' Job 36:23. God's way is his method of working, his manner of governing the world. Now, saith the Holy Ghost, who hath any authority over him, to enjoin him his way of working, the path in which he should walk, that in case he stepped aside, he might say unto him, Thou hast wrought iniquity? No, not any; and therefore it is desperate presumption for any to complain of him whatever he doth: 'Who art thou that repliest against God?' Rom. 9:20. He is a bold man indeed that will contend with his Maker. Who art thou? What manner of man? What monster of men? Who art thou, a clod of clay, a lump of earth, a sink of sin, a firebrand of hell, that thou darest chop logic with God? For shame! sit still, lay thy hand on thy mouth, and be silent.

XIV

GOD INCOMPARABLE IN HIS WORKING; HE DOTH THE GREATEST THINGS WITH EASE, AND WITHOUT ANY HELP

(3). He worketh at all times without weariness, and doth the greatest things with ease. As there is nothing too hard for God, so there is nothing hard to God. He doth the hardest things that are with the greatest ease. Indeed, the great God doth the greatest and hardest things with the same ease that he doth the least things. It is all one to him whether his work be small or great, easy or hard to others; all is easy alike to him.

In the creation, though the building be large and vast, yet with what ease did he set it up! He did not blow or sweat, no, nor so much as stir at his work. The whole world consisteth of the celestial and terrestrial globe, and both were the product of his word. For the heavens: Ps. 33:6, 'By the word of the Lord the heavens were made, and all the host thereof by the breath of his mouth.' It was but a word, a breath, that produced that vast circumference of the heavens, and all those great luminaries there. So for the earth, 'He spake, and it was done; he commanded, and it stood fast,' ver. 9. He only spake the word, and even nonentities obeyed, and became beings. Therefore, in the story of the creation, Gen. 1, we find in every day's work God only commanding, and immediately all things concurring, ver. 3, 9, 12.

In his works of providence he doth all things with inconceivable ease.

If he destroy and pull down, it is done with ease. 'They are crushed as a moth,' Job 4:19. How easily doth a man crush a moth between his fingers! with more ease doth God crush his stoutest enemies. He destroyeth the highest, the greatest, the strongest; the lions, young lions, with a breath, with a blast. 'By the blast of God they perish; by the breath of his nostrils they are consumed,' Job 4:9, 10. By a blast, a breath; it is easy to breathe, to send forth a blast, for a man; but much easier for God, who breathed into man the breath of life. This can put him to no pain, no toil, no trouble at all.

Sennacherib comes against Jerusalem with a great army of warriors, and had, as he saith, counsel and strength for war. God undertakes to deal with him on the behalf of his own people, and to destroy him; but see with what ease God doth it: 2 Kings 19:17, 'I will send a blast upon him.' I will never trouble myself to use my artillery, or draw out my great ordnance of heaven, my thunders and lightnings against so many thousand soldiers; I will only blow upon them, that shall be all.

He destroyeth with a word. If he do but speak, it is done. His saying is doing. 'At what time I speak concerning a nation, to pull down and to destroy,' Jer. 18:7. When the prophet would speak the certain ruin of the Philistines, he doth it in this manner: 'Woe to the inhabitants of the sea coasts, the word of the Lord is against you,' Zeph. 2:5; i.e., The case is woeful, your condition is desperate; the whole world cannot save you, for the 'word of the Lord is against you.' Men may talk and boast, and threaten what they will do, when all the while their words are but wind, and their threatened folk live long; but the word of God, like lightning or mildew, blasteth wherever it goes, and burns up to the very root. Julius Cæsar told Metellus, when he would have prevented his robbing the Roman treasury, Young man, be quiet, or I will lay thee dead at my feet. And then, to magnify his own power, addeth, It is harder for me to speak it than to do it. But this is certain, it is as easy for God to do anything as to speak of it; yea, he doth what he will with a word. Now, how easy is it to speak! He destroyeth with a look, with a glance of his eye; and surely that is easy to him that is all eye, that made the eye. 'In the morning watch the Lord looked through the pillar of fire on the host of the Egyptians, and troubled them,' Exod. 14:24. He darts out beams of death from his eyes. One look from God will take away the life of the greatest of his adversaries. He destroyeth with a hiss. Oh, how little, how easy a thing is hissing: Isa. 7:18, 'I will hiss for the flies of Egypt and the bees of Assyria, and they shall come,' &c.

He destroyeth with a turn of his hand: Ps. 81:13, 14, 'I would soon have subdued their enemies, and turned my hand against them that hated them.' A turn of his hand would have subdued the proudest enemies of Israel, and have stabbed them to the heart.

He delivereth his people with the greatest ease. Whatsoever their straits be, though various and difficult, yet he helpeth them out with ease. When they were in captivity, scattered up and down as exiles out of their own country, he bringeth them home. But how? Truly, 'He saith to the north, give up; and to the south, keep not back,' &c., Isa. 43:6. And both hearken to his word, that his 'sons come from far, and his daughters from the ends of the earth.' When the prophet would beg of him to help his afflicted people, he only desires him to 'command deliverance for Jacob,' Ps. 44:4. If he will it, and command it, the work is done.

He succeedeth his ordinances, and maketh them effectual for enlightening the blind and enlivening the dead (great works) with ease.

He saith, Live, and the dead sinner liveth, John 5:24. He commandeth success, and ordinances are effectual. 'There the Lord commandeth his blessing, even life forevermore,' Ps. 133:3.

Yea, the ocean, that is such a frightful monster, which makes such a horrible noise, and openeth its mouth, roaring and raging, as if it would certainly devour us, is quelled and quieted with ease by him, Job 38:8–11. When the sea was tempestuous, and frighted the disciples that they awake the Lord Jesus, with what ease doth he cause a calm, 'Peace, be still,' Mat. 8:27; as a mother would still a crying child: Hush, be quiet, peace, no more, be still; and 'immediately there was a calm.'

(4). He worketh wholly by his own power, without the least help from any other. Creatures are all instruments, and act in the virtue of the principal efficient. Angels and men act not in their own, but in the strength of God; they have not some help from God, but all the power by which they work from God. But God acteth wholly in his own strength, he never had nor desired a helping hand from any of his creatures.

In the work of creation he erected this curious large fabric without any tool or instrument: Isa. 44:24, 'I am the Lord that made all things, that stretcheth forth the heavens alone, that spreadeth abroad the earth by myself.' Mark, he made the heavens alone, had none with him to assist him; and he made the earth by himself, called none from heaven to his aid. As he said to Job, 'Where wast thou when I laid the foundations of the earth? Declare, if thou hast understanding,' Job 38:4. Thou wast far enough off from giving any help. So he may say to angels, 'Where were ye when I stretched out the heavens? Declare, if ye have unstanding.' Some give that reason why they are not mentioned in the creation of the world, in the first of Genesis, to assure us, that God did not use their help in his work. The heavens are compared to a curtain, Ps. 104, and to a tent, Isa. 40:22. Now we know that when curtains or tents that are very large, are to be stretched out, as the phrase is in that Isa. 44:24, there needs many hands to it, one hand will not do it, many pair of hands must be put to it, but God spreadeth out those wide large curtains of heaven alone, Job 9:8. He borrowed not one hand to it: 'Hast thou with him spread out the sky, which is strong as a molten looking-glass?' Job 37:18. Was God beholden to thee for affording him thine arms in the unfolding and spreading that broad vast piece?

In works of providence he doth some great things alone by himself: Job 26:7, 'He hangeth the earth on nothing,' without an Atlas to bear it up; and he preserves Moses forty days without food, Exod. 32. And he doth all things without the help of his creatures, even there and then when he makes the most use of his creatures. He useth angels and men in the government of the world; he useth many means, as food and raiment, and physic and sleep, for the preservation of our health and lives; but he doth all as much and as surely as if he made not use of any means at all. He is the soul of the world, that actuates everything in it; hence we read, that instruments are called his sword, Ps. 17:14; his rod, Isa. 10:5. What can the sword or the rod do without a hand to cut or scourge with them? Therefore when his rod boasteth as if it could scourge of itself, Isa. 10:12, 13, and as if it were the hand too, 'By the strength of my hand have I done it; I have removed the bounds of the people, and robbed their treasure;' God quickly contradicts such vain babbling, and confutes such vainglorious boasting: ver. 15, 'Shall the axe boast itself against him that heweth therewith, or the saw magnify itself against him that shaketh it?' Thou poor proud vain-glorious wretch, thou art a mere axe, a saw, and canst no more move or cut of thyself than a saw or an axe that lieth on the ground, which no man meddleth with. Thou talkest arrogantly and saucily, as if thou didst all when thou didst nothing; I did all, thou wast all the while but the axe and saw in my hand, which I made use of.

Whether God have little or great means, means or no means, it is all one to him; there is not a pin to choose, as we say, for he doth as much when he hath means as when he hath none: 2 Chron. 14:11, 'It is all one with thee to help with many, or with them that have no power.' It is not the least difference to him, it is not so much as the smallest dust in the balance to turn the scale of victory, whether God have many or few, any or none on[28] his side.

God never made use of any creatures because he had the least need of them, or the least help by them, but partly because it is his pleasure; he useth them because he will use them: It is his pleasure 'by the foolishness of preaching to save them that believe,' 1 Cor. 1:21; not that he hath the least aid from preachers. So it is his pleasure by food and sleep to preserve man's life; not that he hath any help from them: 'Thy visitation preserveth

---

[28] Text: of.

my spirit,' Job 10:12. Partly from his own honour. Hereby he magnifieth his sovereignty, and sheweth his dominion over all his creatures, that they are all at his beck, and he can with a stamp of his foot, or a glance of his eye, or a hiss of his mouth, call them from the uttermost parts of the world, to execute his command: 'My hand hath laid the foundations of the earth, my right hand hath spanned the heavens; when I call they stand up together,' Isa. 48:13. The flies, caterpillars, locusts, stars in their courses, &c., all come at his call. Hereby he magnifieth his power, that can do such great things by weak means. He got himself glory on Pharaoh, when he made pitiful contemptible creatures, as lice and flies, such plagues to him.

And by opening the eyes of the blind, and quickening the dead, by such weak poor instruments as men are, his strength is exceedingly exalted: 'We have this treasure in earthen vessels, that the excellency of the power might be of God,' 2 Cor. 4:7. Hereby he magnifieth his wisdom, viz., in discovering the fitness and aptitude of his creatures to those ends and purposes for which they were created. The use of a tool discovers its worth, by discovering its serviceableness to that for which it was made. Partly to endear creatures one to another; their mutual serviceableness each to other, causeth the greater amity and unity between them, 1 Cor. 12:21-23.

In spiritual things also God worketh alone, even when he hath many ordinances and ministers to serve him: 'Thou workest all our works in us, and for us,' Isa. 26:12. Not any visions, or prophets, or industry of our own, but thou workest all. What is Paul? What is Apollos? Paul planteth, Apollos watereth, but God giveth the increase. So then, observe, he that planteth is—a great apostle? No—nothing, and he that watereth is—an eloquent excellent person? No—nothing, but God that giveth the increase, 1 Cor. 3:5–7. God doth not use preachers because they help him in the conversion of souls; but, as I said before, because it his pleasure, 1 Cor. 1:21; and he turneth it to his honour, 2 Cor. 4:7; therefore it is often seen that ministers of the largest gifts, of the greatest grace, are not often the most successful in their labours; because God would have us know, that it is not the parts or piety of the preacher, but his grace and Spirit that doth the work; they are nothing, he is all in all. He made light the first day of the creation, and not the sun or stars till the fourth, to tell the world that he can enlighten it without the sun. It is a great honour to God that he hath so many millions of creatures at his will and pleasure, that he hath so many eyes to see for him, and so many ears to hear for him, and so many hands to work for him;

but it is a greater honour to him that he needeth none of them, he can do all without them; that though they are serviceable to him, yet they are not necessary to him; for God and all his creatures do no more, can do no more than God without any of his creatures.

XV

GOD IS INCOMPARABLE IN HIS WORD; HE SPEAKETH WITH INCOMPARABLE AUTHORITY, CONDESCENSION, AND EFFICACY

IV. Fourthly, God is incomparable in his word; he speaketh after an unspeakable manner: 'Never man spake like him,' no, nor angels, his enemies themselves being judges, John 7:46. Men may speak high, and speak holily; angels may speak higher and holier, but neither speak like God: 'Behold, he exalteth by his power; who teacheth like him?' Job 36:22. Behold, wonder at it, he exalteth by his power, is good at acting; 'Who teacheth like him?' is good at instructing, and best at both, and beyond all that ever were; 'Who teacheth like him?' The words are a challenge to the whole world. Bring forth the man, let me see the angel, that can speak or teach like God. He doth not say, Who teacheth beside God? There are many teachers beside God: the inanimate creatures are teachers, the heavens by their constant regular motion, the earth by its fecundity and fruitfulness, according to the law of their creation, teach man obedience and proficiency, Isa. 48:13. The irrational creatures are teachers; man is sent to school to the ant and swallow, and ox and ass, to the beasts of the field, and the fowls of the air, to learn providence and prudence; to learn wisdom, to discern and improve his opportunities, and gratitude to his Father and benefactor, Prov. 6:6; Jer. 7:7, 8; Isa. 1:5; Job 12:8, 9. Men are teachers one to another. Parents and ministers do, or should, teach those that are committed to their charge or trust, Prov. 22:6; Eph. 4:6. Angels are teachers: the angel taught Daniel, and helped him to understand, Dan. 10:14; and surely of all finite, they are the most learned and able masters: but he saith, Who teacheth like him? Though many teach beside God, yet none teacheth like God; none speaketh like him, whether you consider the manner, the matter, or the effect of his speech.

1. He is incomparable in the manner of his speaking.

(1). He speaketh authoritatively, and in his own name. Good men and good angels may command, but it must be as subordinate magistrates, in the name and authority of their prince and sovereign; but God commandeth in his own name and authority; God gives authenticity to whatever he speaks, and he speaks with authority when he speaks. God speaks as one that hath right and power to command, and as one that, upon his own account, expecteth to be obeyed: I am the Lord, is enough to warrant obedience to the whole decalogue. 'Thou shalt have no other God; thou shalt not make to thyself any graven image, &c., for I am the Lord thy God.'

His authority is the highest, the greatest reason of any precept, and the strongest warrant for obedience: 'Therefore thou shalt not swear by my name falsely,' why? 'I am the Lord.' 'Thou shalt not curse the deaf, nor lay a stumbling-block before the blind;' why not? The deaf cannot hear if I do curse them, nor the blind see if I do lay a stumbling-block before them; 'I am the Lord,' &c., Lev. 19:12, &c. It is said of Christ, 'He taught as one having authority, and not as the scribes,' Mat. 7:29. He did not beg attention, but enjoin it; nor beseech obedience, but command it. As when princes enact laws, they do not entreat, but require obedience at the peril of their subjects. This is the word of the Lord, and Thus saith the Lord, and The mouth of the Lord hath spoken it, is sufficient to awe and require subjection from all that hear it. God is his own authority, not so men or angels; they speak from God, but he from none but himself. His word is a light, Ps. 119:104, 105, that discovers itself; and therefore it is called 'The testimony of the Lord,' Ps. 19:7; because it beareth witness to itself, and needeth not testimony from men or angels. What the essential Word speaketh may be spoken of the declarative word: it receiveth not testimony from man, John 5:34. Men need grounds and reasons, and witnesses too, to prove and vouch what they say to be true, and to be so as they speak; but the word of God is a sufficient authentic testimony to itself; it is his own proof, because what truth itself speaks must of necessity be true.

(2). He speaketh condescendingly to the condition and understanding of those to whom he speaketh; he considereth the natures and tempers and capacities of his hearers, and accordingly speaks to them; he doth not, as some ministers, speak in an unknown tongue, or soar into the clouds, exceed the capacities of his hearers, that he might be wondered at, not understood; but he observeth their weakness and infirmities, yea, their dulness and incapacity, and teacheth them as they are able to hear him. There are depths in his word for elephants to swim in—to tell the world what and how he could speak, to exercise our industry, and prevent our contempt of it for its plainness—and there are shallows for lambs to wade through, that none might be discouraged. Christ is our priest, and the priest's lips teach knowledge, and he is a merciful priest, Heb. 2:16. Condescending in what he teacheth, and in the way of his teaching, to the capacities of his hearers.

In what he teacheth. How chary was Christ of charging his disciples with anything that they could not brook: John 16:12, 'I have many things to say unto you, but ye cannot hear them now.' I have some harder lessons to teach you, but ye are young scholars, and not able yet to learn them, till ye have been longer in my school, and have attained more ripeness of understanding; therefore I will not trouble you now with them, but leave them to my Spirit, who shall prepare you for them, and enable you to learn them: your stomachs are weak, and yet must have that only which is of light digestion—milk, not strong meat, 1 Cor. 3:2. Your backs are not strong, and therefore I will lay on you none but light burdens, but ye cannot bear them now, and therefore ye shall not hear them now, lest ye should be offended and discouraged at them. When the Jews inquired of Christ why his disciples did not fast often, as well as the disciples of John and the Pharisees: observe the reason our tender-hearted Lord gives,

Mat. 9:16, 17, 'No man,' saith he, 'puts new wine into old bottles, lest the wine burst the bottles; or seweth an old garment to new cloth, lest the rent be worse.' Alas, saith he, my disciples are young beginners, babes in me, at best but little children, not strong men, or fathers, and therefore they must not be called presently to the austerities or severities of religion, lest they, poor souls, should be discouraged in their work, and faint under it; I must proportion their burden to their backs, and lead them their own pace as they are able to go at present. Hereafter indeed they shall be called to suffer great things for my name's sake; they shall be hated and persecuted of all men, but then they shall be fitted for those severities, and undergo them with courage; but yet such deep points, and obscure notions, must not be offered to novices.

In the way of his teaching he is very tender and condescending; he accommodates his discourse to their apprehension: Mark 4:33, 'He spake as they were able to bear it;' not as he was able to speak, (he was able to read lectures above the capacities of angels,) but 'as they were able to bear it;' therefore, he spake so much to them in parables, because they might the better understand him: for though a parable would make truth more obscure—and so parables and dark sayings are conjoined, Ps. 78:2, and to speak in parables is opposed to speaking plainly, John 16:25, 29— yet a parable revealed, unveiled, as Christ did usually to his disciples, Mat. 13:17, 37, makes truth more clear. It gives us the advantage of viewing heavenly truth in earthly glasses, the species and reflections of which we are most able to conceive; therefore our Saviour saith, 'If I have told you earthly things, and ye believe not, (or cannot understand,) how shall ye believe if I tell you of heavenly?' John 3:12.

The instructions of Christ were like water, Deut. 32:2, which he poured into those narrow-mouthed vessels by little and little, as they were able to receive it; or as rain, which he distilled on his hearers, as rain on the mown grass, by drops, and drop after drop, to refresh them; not by floods to drown them. Jacob considered the children were young, and the cattle were with young, therefore drove gently, lest by overdriving he should wrong them, Gen. 33:13. So our Lord Jesus considereth what men are, how impotent and infirm, and will not overdrive, overdo, lest he should undo them: Isa. 28:10, 'He gives precept upon precept, line upon line; here a little, there a little.'

Will men or angels teach with such compassion, with such condescension? It is a rule of one of the ancients, that he who will teach children, must himself be a child. He must frame and fashion himself to them, and be as one of them, or else he will never teach them. How soon would the dulness and untowardness of man tire out the patience of men and angels, and provoke them to give over teaching them! God's incomparableness herein is fully proved in the incomparableness of God in his patience, in chap. 10.

(3). He speaks effectually. As he hath power to command us, so he hath power to enable us to obey his commands. Men and angels may tell men their duty, but they cannot teach men their duty; they cannot strengthen them, or empower them to obey. He speaketh so as men hear, and believe and live: 'He that heard and learned of the Father, cometh unto me,' John 6:45. We have a saying, *Ex quovis ligno non fit Mercurius*, Every man will not make a Mercury. Some so dull and blockish, that none can improve them, or do good upon them, Isa. 32:4, i.e., no creature can; but God can make the dull, the blind, the most ignorant, to conceive and consider, and apprehend and understand the darkest and most difficult points by speaking to them: Isa. 48:17, He teacheth to profit. There is a power that accompanieth his teaching, that doth the work. When he saith, Let there be light in a dark mind, there is light; it is so. He is a God that commandeth light to shine out of darkness, 2 Cor. 4:6. When he saith. Let there be life in that dead soul, there is life; it is so, John 5:24. Men and angels may call long enough to the blind to see, and the dead to live, and all in vain. But if a God say to a sinner that lieth rotting in the grave, almost eaten up of the vermin of lusts, unsavoury, and stinking in the eyes of all men, Lazarus, sinner, come forth of thy cursed carnal condition; the man that was bound hand and foot, manacled and fettered by the devil, his jailer, comes forth, is loosed of his bonds, and lives forever.

As the mariners said of Christ, He speaketh with authority, and commandeth the winds and seas, and they obey him; what manner of man is this? Mat. 8:27: so I may say, Oh what manner of God is this, for he speaks with authority, and the high winds of violent passions, and the fierce waters of boisterous corruptions, and they obey him; they fly, they fall before him! Can men or angels speak at this rate? Will sin die at their word? Will the soul live at their command? How long may they call to sinners to arise from the dead, before they will, before they can answer their call!

But if God speaks, the most obstinate hardened sinner obeyeth his voice, submitteth to his will, and yieldeth himself up to his word; nay, the very devils are forced to leave their beloved mansions, the souls of men, and to seek and settle their habitations elsewhere. He commandeth, and the unclean spirits come out of men, Mat. 8:32. If he please but to say. Get thee behind me, Satan, that prince of the powers of the air, that god of the world, who crows so much on his own dunghill, the hearts of the unregenerate, sneaks away like a coward, and must in spite of his teeth obey his command. Mat. 4:10, 11; yea, God ejecteth him with a word speaking, out of his strongest holds, the souls of old, senseless, seared sinners, and leads captivity captive, and makes this jailer, who laid so many in irons, his prisoner and captive.

XVI

GOD IS INCOMPARABLE IN HIS WORD: IN ITS PURITY, MYSTERIES, PROPHECIES

2. God is incomparable in the matter of his speech, as well as in his manner of speaking; if you consider the purity, mysteries, or predictions thereof.

(1). The purity of its precepts. His word is the most pure, perfect, exact rule of righteousness that is imaginable. It commandeth good, nothing but good, and all good, at all times; it forbiddeth evil, all evil, and nothing but evil, and always: 'The commandment is holy, and the law is holy, just, and good,' Rom. 7:12. Holy, as it is a copy of the divine will; just, as it is correspondent to the highest reason; good, as it is most beneficial to the rational creature. It is holy, as it relates to our duty to God; just, as it respects our duty to our neighbours; good, as it concerns our duty towards ourselves. It is holy, as consecrated to the service of God; just, as a transcript of the pure law of nature; good, as it is the measure and standard of all goodness in the creatures. It is holy in what it enjoins us to do; just in what it forbids us to do; and good in both. What laws in the world are in any degree comparable to the laws of God? The Mohammedan laws, which have gained so much credit in the greatest part almost of the known world, are impure laws, allowing revenge, polygamy, and commanding slaughters, oppressions, &c., for the propagation of their religion.

The laws of the severest heathen, Lycurgus, &c., contained but the carcase and body of purity, had nothing of the soul and life thereof. How many sins against the very law of nature did that Lacedemonian lawgiver allow of! And where he or any of the rest did forbid sin, it was in the outward actions, not in the inward affections. Their laws did rather command the covering of sin, that it might not appear abroad, than the killing of sin, that it might not be at all. Their laws were defective as to persons; some men were usually privileged, and not bound to them; as to the parts of men, they gave the inward man liberty, though they restrained the outward as to punishments; the greatest penalty they could think of or impose, was a temporal death. They never dreamed of a hell in another world. But oh how pure, how perfect is the law of God! 'Thy word is very pure,' saith David, Ps. 119. So pure, that there is not the least mixture, falsehood, or error in it. It commands all, and nothing but conformity to the mind of the great sovereign, and Lord of all things: 'The law of the Lord is perfect,' Ps. 19:7. So perfect, that it is not deficient in anything. It commandeth purity in the whole man, in every faculty of the soul, in every member of the body. It commandeth purity in this whole man, at all times, in all companies, in all conditions, in all relations, in all manner of conversation, 1 Pet. 1:15, 16: Ps. 119:1, 2.

It is apparent to common sense, that fallen man could never dream of such strict exact precepts; no, he is so far from it, that he is wholly contrary thereunto, Rom. 8:7. And angels could not imagine them, unless God had signified his mind to them. For all holiness being a conformity to the will of the Most High God, they could not discern what was holy, what was unholy, any further then they could discover the will of this incomparable God.

(2). The mystery of its doctrines. It containeth such depths, such bottomless profundities, that could not possibly have been imagined by men or angels, had not God revealed them. It acquainteth us with things far above the reach of created reason, though not contrary; yet being told us are so correspondent, that there is no ground left for the questioning them. What the great apostle saith upon occasion of one mystery, we may say upon the whole: Oh the depth, 'Oh the depth of the wisdom and knowledge of God,' Rom. 11:33. Oh the depth of the Holy Scriptures. There is a depth in them that none can fathom, because a depth in them that hath no bottom. Great is the mystery of the Bible. Who could think of a woman's coming into the world without a woman, as Eve; of a man's coming into the world without a man, as the Son of man; nay, without man or woman, as Adam? Who could think that the same woman should be a mother and a virgin? But these are small mysteries; who could think that many thousands, millions, living many miles and ages distant, should be fellow—members, and be truly one body, sympathising with, serviceable to, rejoicing in the welfare of each other, and all be united unto, receive influence from, and live wholly by one head, as far from them as heaven is from the earth?

Eph. 5:27–30; Col. 2:19. Who could have thought that three really and personally distinct should be equal, and one in nature and essence? 1 John 5:7.

Who could have imagined that God should become man, infinite become finite, the Creator a creature; the Father of spirits become flesh, and the Lord of life be put to death? Who could conceive, that he who made all things of nothing, should be made himself of a woman, made by him? That he whom the heavens, and heaven of heavens cannot contain, should be contained in the narrow womb of a woman? That the only bread of life should be hungry, the only water of life be thirsty; the only rest be weary, the only ease be pained, and the only joy and consolation be sorrowful, exceeding sorrowful unto death?

Who could have imagined that one, yea, millions, should be rich by another's poverty, filled by another's emptiness, be exalted by another's disgrace, healed by another's wounds, eased by another's pains, be absolved by another's condemnation, and live eternally by another's temporal death? Who could have imagined that infinite justice and infinite mercy should be made fast friends, and fully satisfied by one and the same action; that the greatest fury and the greatest favour, the greatest hatred and the greatest love, should concur in, and be manifested by one and the same thing? Could men or angels speak such mysteries? Surely no. Several mysteries in the Scriptures were hid from whole ages and generations of men: 'Which in former ages was not made known to the children of men,' Eph. 3:5. No nor to angels neither: ver. 10, 'To the intent that now unto principalities and powers might be made known by the church the manifold wisdom of God.'

(3). The prophecies and predictions of the word. Neither men nor angels can foretell those things which depend not on natural causes, or which may not be deduced from moral or political grounds; and even in such things as these are, they may be, and have been deceived. Therefore it was the subtlety of the old serpent to deliver his oracles often in ambiguous words and in deceitful speeches, that whatsoever happened, his credit might be saved, as his *Aio te Æacida, Romanos vincere posse,* and *Ibis, redibis, nunquam per bella peribis,*[29] &c. But God foretells what hath no print of any footing in nature, what neither moral nor political principles can

---

[29] This saying, delivered by the Delphic oracle to Phyrrus, king of Egypt, has two possible translations: "I say that you, descendant of Aeacus, are able to conquer Rome. You shall go, you shall return, you shall never perish in war;" and, "I say that Rome is able to conquer you, descendant of Aeacus. You shall go, you shall never return, you shall perish in war."

direct unto, and never fails in his predictions. He foretells the birth of Cyrus one hundred years before he was born Isa. 44:28; the birth of Josiah, two hundred years, 1 Kings 13:2; the conversion of the Gentiles, and falling off of the Jews, above two thousand years before it came to pass, Gen. 9:27; Isa. 49:6, and 54:9, 10. He foretells the birth of Christ near four thousand years before he came into the world, Gen. 3:15. And it is very observable how punctual and particular he is herein, as knowing how much the welfare of the world did depend upon the knowledge of the true Messiah: he tells you long beforehand of what tribe he should come, of Judah; of what family, David's; of what person, a virgin; where he should be born, in Bethlehem; whence he must be called, out of Egypt; what his condition should be in general, full of sorrows and griefs; in particular, that he should be disgraced and reviled, tempted, betrayed, apprehended, deserted by his Father and brethren; that he should die, be pierced, not have a bone broken; be buried; make his grave with the rich and the wicked, and rise again from the dead, and reap the fruit of all his passion to his full satisfaction.

He hath foretold the state of the world and the church in the Revelation, from the primitive times to the dissolution of the world, though it is written in shorthand and in dark characters.

And can any men or angels foretell such things? God challengeth all the gods to do this: 'Shew the things that are to come hereafter, that we may know that ye are gods,' Isa. 41:21–23. The certain prediction of future contingents is such an inseparable prerogative of the Deity, and such a special privilege of the Original of all things, that he engageth to own their supremacy and acknowledge their sovereignty who can do it. It is such a jewel in his crown, that none ever shared in it: 'I have declared the former things from the beginning: I did them suddenly, and they came to pass: I have even from the beginning declared it to thee; before it came to pass, I shewed it to thee,' Isa. 48:3, 5. It is peculiar to him, who worketh all in all, to foreknow and foretell whatsoever shall come to pass: Acts 15:18, 'Known to God are all his works, from the beginning of the world,' yea, from all eternity. For he stood on the high mountain of eternity, and thence had a full view of all that his will would produce, and whatsoever should come to pass.

XVII

GOD INCOMPARABLE IN HIS WORD, AS IT IS CONVERTING, AFFRIGHTING, AND COMFORTING

3. God is incomparable in the effects of his word. His words are works; they are operative, as well as declarative of his pleasure. What he speaketh hath power and virtue in it, as well as weight and value.

(1). It is efficacious in converting the soul. The word of God can stop the tide of nature, when it runneth with the greatest violence; yea, it can turn it the quite contrary way. Let a man be in the height of his strength, in the heat of his youth, ruffling and bustling among the sparks of the times, taking a large draught of carnal pleasures, and having a full gust of sensual delights, making his whole life but a diversion from one pleasure to another, as if he were sent into the earth, as leviathan into the waters, only to play and sport there; when this man is in his best estate, in the zenith of health and strength, in the meridian of his age, promising himself a long day of life, and putting the day of death far from him, and thereby giving himself the more liberty to the service of his lusts, yet if the word of God come to this man, who sucketh in wind as the wild ass's colt, it makes him pluck in his plumes, bid adieu to his foolish pleasures, leave his most beloved lusts, loathe himself forever loving them. It alters the man's palate; that is bitter now which was sweet before, and he cannot savour what formerly was his heaven and happiness; it changeth the bent and frame of his heart, that now he forsaketh with detestation what formerly he followed after as his only felicity and chiefest good. The wild man is tame, the obstinate man is pliable, and the distracted man is recovered to his wits, Ps. 119:9. Men and angels may persuade, but God only can prevail. The words of creatures may work for an outward reformation, but the word of God alone for an inward renovation. He only that made the heart can mend it. Human counsels may do somewhat towards the hiding of the corruptions of nature, but divine instructions are only effectual for the healing of corrupted nature: 'The law of the Lord is perfect, converting the soul,' Ps. 19:7.

Converting the soul: The law of man may bind the body to its good behaviour, but the law of God alone can bring the soul to its good behaviour. To turn a lion into a lamb, darkness into light, a stone into flesh, death into life, all which is done in conversion, can be effected by the word of none but God, Isa. 11:8–10; Eph. 5:8; Ezek. 26; Eph. 2:1, 5. No word but his can take a scion off from its own natural stock, and engraft it into a new stock, Rom. 11:17; James 1:21; 2 Cor. 10:4; Acts 2:41, and 4:4.

(2). It is efficacious in affrighting the sinner. He speaks, not as men or angels, to the ears only, but to the hidden man of the heart, and shatters it in pieces. He plants his batteries of threatenings, and terrors, and curses, against the inward man of the conscience, and puts it into an ague of trembling and shaking fits, as we see in Herod, Acts 24:27, and levels it to the ground. This word, in the mouth of a poor prisoner at the bar, frights the proud sturdy judge on the bench. When God speaks, he makes the best people afraid, and cry out, Let not God speak to us, lest we die, and the best of that people exceedingly to quake and fear, Exod. 19:19; Heb. 12:21: 'The voice of the Lord is terrible, it shaketh the cedars of Lebanon, it shattereth the oaks of Bashan,' Ps. 29. Those that were monsters of mankind for cruelty and barbarousness, for stupidity and searedness, by his word have been terrified in their spirits, wounded in their consciences, cut to the heart, and forced to call out, 'Sirs, what shall we do to be saved?' Acts 2:37.

The most stubborn, senseless sinner, whom neither mercies nor miseries could move or melt, who mocked at the curses of the law and the wrath of the Lord, and as leviathan laughed at the shaking of those spears, whom, as the man possessed with the devil, no cords could hold, no chains could fasten, but he burst all asunder, when the word of the Lord hath been spoken to him, instead of flying in his face, as formerly, when men have spoken to him, he hath fallen down at his feet, been filled with fears and frights, felt the very fire of hell flaming in his conscience, and become a very Magor Missabib,[30] fear or terror to himself round about. The word of God hath stuck in his heart, as the arrow in the side of the buck, allowing no ease whithersoever he hath gone; in the night, scaring him with dreams, and terrifying him with visions; in the day admitting no rest in his flesh, nor quietness in his bones; forcing him in all places, and in all companies, still

---

[30] A transliteration of the Hebrew phrase meaning "terror on every side" from Jeremiah 20:3, "tocks, Jeremiah said to him, "The LORD does not call your name Pashhur, but Terror on Every Side."

to carry his jailer, his tormentor, his executioner along with him; and at last, that he might escape a partial and temporal, to leap into a total, an eternal hell. Ah, who knoweth the power of his anger? Of his angry word, or is able to fear him according to his wrath? Ps. 90:11. I may challenge every man, every angel, as God himself doth Job, 'Hast thou an arm like God? Canst thou thunder with thy voice like him?' Job 40:9. If he utter his word of fury, the rocks are rent in pieces, the most stony hearts are melted; the mountains are moved, the highest and firmliest-seated sinners are shaken out of their places and senses, the foundations of the world tremble and quake, the strongest pillars are troubled, the whole frame and body of nature is affected with a palsy: Ps. 18:13, 'The Lord thundered in the heavens, the Highest gave forth his voice;' what followeth? 'hail-stones and coals of fire.'

(3). It is efficacious in healing the wounded spirit. When God takes the sword of the Spirit into his own hand, and wields it with his own arm, it makes work, it makes wounds to purpose in the consciences of men; the sleepy soul is now awakened, the secure soul is now affrighted, the senseless soul is now affected with his sins and misery, Acts 2:37; the man tasteth the bitterness of his original and actual corruptions, feeleth the weight of divine fury and indignation, findeth the poison to work in his bowels, and racking him with extremity of pain. There is no rest in his flesh, because of God's anger; nor quiet in his bones, because of his sins. The arrows of the Almighty are within him, and his terrors set themselves in array against him, Ps. 38:4; Job 6:10. The unquenchable fire flasheth in his face, and destruction (in his thoughts) is ready to lay hold of him; in this condition he knoweth not what to do, for a 'wounded spirit who can bear?' Prov. 18:14. He trieth creatures, but they can afford him no ease; miserable comforters are they all to him, and physicians of no value. It is the same hand that wounded that alone can cure him; it is the same word that bruised him that must bind him up; let God but speak to this soul that is thus sunk down into hell, and it will be lifted up to heaven. 'Fools, because of their iniquities and transgressions, are afflicted, their soul abhorreth all manner of meat,' (they are so sick that they can relish, take down nothing,) 'and they draw near to the gates of death,' they are almost in, they are on the brink of hell; what course must be used for their cure? Truly this, 'He sent his word and healed them, and delivered them from their destruction,' Ps. 107:17–20. No herb in the garden of the whole world can do these distressed creatures the least good. Friends may speak, and ministers may speak, yea, angels may speak, and yet all in vain; the wounds are incurable for all their words; but if God please to speak, the dying soul reviveth. His word is the only balm that can cure the wounded conscience; 'he sendeth his word and healeth them.' Conscience is God's prisoner, he claps it in hold, he layeth it in fetters, that the iron enters the very soul; this he doth by his word, and truly he only who shuts up can let out; all the world cannot open the iron gate, knock off the shackles, and set the poor prisoner at liberty, till God speak the word.

David professed, he had quite fainted, had it not been for this *aqua vitæ*,[31] this cordial water: 'I had perished in my affliction, but thy word comforted me,' Ps. 119:92. The boisterous billows went over my soul, and I had sunk in those deep waters, had not thy word borne me up.

---

[31] "Water of life."

II

APPLICATION OF GOD'S INCOMPARABLENESS

XVIII

IF GOD BE INCOMPARABLE, 1. HOW GREAT IS THE MALIGNITY OF SIN, WHICH CONTEMNETH, DISHONOURETH, AND OPPOSETH THIS GOD!

I come now to make some application of this great and weighty truth; it may be useful by way of information, counsel, and comfort.

I. First, By way of information. If God be so incomparable, that there is none on earth, none in heaven comparable to him, it may inform us,

1. Of the great venom and malignity of sin, because it is an injury to so great, so glorious, so incomparable a being. The higher and better any object is, the baser and the worse is that action which is injurious to it. To throw dirt on sackcloth is not so bad as to throw dirt on scarlet or fine linen. To make a flaw in a pebble or common stone is nothing to the making a flaw in a diamond or precious stone. Those opprobrious speeches, or injurious actions, against an ordinary person, which are but a breach of the good behaviour, and bear but a common action at law, if against a prince, may be high treason, because of the excellency of his place, and majesty of his person. The worth and dignity of the object doth exceedingly heighten and aggravate the offence. How horrid then is sin, and of how heinous a nature, when it offendeth and opposeth not kings, the highest of men, not angels, the highest of creatures, but God, the highest of beings; the incomparable God, to whom kings and angels, yea, the whole creation is less than nothing! We take the size of sin too low, and short, and wrong, when we measure it by the wrong it doth to ourselves, or our families, or our neighbours, or the nation wherein we live; indeed, herein somewhat of its evil and mischief doth appear; but to take its full length and proportion, we must consider the wrong it doth to this great, this glorious, this incomparable God. Sin is incomparably malignant, because the God principally injured by it is incomparably excellent. It is one thing to displease and offend man, a poor slimy worm, a mean shallow creature, of the same make and

mould with ourselves; and another thing to displease and offend God, that unconceiveable immense being: 'If one man sin against another, the judge shall judge him,' (a human judge may undertake to determine and comprise offences between them that stand upon the same level,) 'but if a man sin against the Lord, who shall entreat for him?' 1 Sam. 2:25. Here the case is altered, here is a pitiful finite creature offending an infinite Creator; what man dares arbitrate this difference, nay, who can intercede and interpose between these two?

Hence, hence it is that there is no less than an infinite demerit in sin, because it is an injury to an infinite majesty. Nothing discovers sin to be so great an evil, as its opposition to so vast, so matchless, so great a good, so incomparable a God.

The evil of sin appeareth somewhat in the injury it doth to our estates; 'The drunkard and glutton shall come to poverty, and idleness shall clothe a man with rags,' Prov. 23:21: to our names; 'The name of the wicked shall rot,' Prov. 11:7: to our families; 'A wicked man troubleth his own house,' Prov. 15:27, and 3:33: to our neighbours; 'One sinner destroyeth much good,' Eccles. 3:18: to our nation; Jer. 18:7, 8; Ps. 107:34, 'He turneth a fruitful land into barrenness, for the wickedness of them that dwell therein:' to our bodies; 'Who hath woe? Who hath sorrow? Who hath wounds without cause? They that tarry long at the wine,' Prov. 23:29, 30, and 5:11: to our souls; 'He that sinneth against me wrongeth his own soul,' Prov. 8:36. But all this discovers nothing of sin's evil, to that which is discovered by the injury it doth to the incomparable God, because our estates, our names, our families, our neighbours, our nations, our bodies, our souls are all nothing, infinitely less than nothing, to the great God, the incomparable. This, this is the only glass that discovers the horrid ugly features, the monstrous frightful deformities of sin's face, that it is a wrong to the blessed God, to him who is the high and lofty One, Isa. 57:15.

(1). In that sin is a breach of this incomparable God's law, a violation of his command, a contradiction of his will: 'Whosoever sinneth transgresseth the law, for sin is a transgression of the law,' 1 John 3:4. Neither the greatness nor smallness of our obedience or disobedience is to be valued according to the greatness or smallness of the thing commanded or forbidden, nor according to the greatness or smallness of the good or hurt done to man by it, but according to the greatness of the person who commandeth or forbiddeth.

(2). In that it is a contempt of this incomparable God's authority, a slighting his dominion, a denying his sovereignty: 'Who is the Lord, that I should obey his voice?' Exod. 5:2, is the voice of every sinner. 'We are our own, say they; who is Lord over us?' Ps. 12:4. They know no maker, and therefore own no master. For this cause the sinner is said to cast the incomparable God behind his back, as not worth minding or regarding, 1 Kings 14:9; and to despise him as some mean inconsiderable being, 1 Sam. 2:30; 2 Sam. 12:9, 10.

(3). In that it is a dishonouring this incomparable God, whose name alone is excellent. It layeth him low, who is the Most High, Ps. 92:1: 'Through breaking the law dishonourest thou God?' Rom. 2:23, 24. It is ill to reproach a common man, worse to reproach a nobleman or a prince; but oh, how bad is it to reproach the great God! to blaspheme that worthy name. Sin layeth the honour of this incomparable God, which is more worth than millions of worlds, in the dust, and trampleth on it. The Romans, when they would mark one with ignominy, and brand him with reproach, would put him out of their senate, or any place of credit in which he was, and pull down his statue or monument, if any were erected to his honour. Sin degrades and dethrones God, it will not allow him to be the Lord and supreme of the world, and it defaceth his image wherever it finds it, as one contrary expels another; it disgraceth his justice, thence is called unrighteousness, 1 John 1:6; his wisdom, thence is called folly, Prov. 5:23; his patience, thence is called murmuring, Jude 16; his power, thence is called weakness, Rom. 5:8; his mercy, thence is called unthankfulness, Luke 6:35; his knowledge, thence is called ignorance, and a work of darkness, 1 Pet. 1:14; Eph. 5:8; his truth, thence is called a lie, and lying vanity, Ps. 58:2; Jonah 2:8. In all these, and every way, it disgraceth his holiness, which is his glory, and the glory of all his attributes, Exod. 15:11, thence is called filthiness, 2 Cor. 7:1; uncleanness, Rom. 1:24.

(4). In that it is a fighting with, and to its power, a destroying this incomparable God. The murder of any man is heinous, it is horrid, it is against nature, and it is the extremest mischief that one creature can do to another, Gen. 4:10; Mat. 10:28. The murder of a father or a sovereign is far more heinous, as being more against nature, and against more engagements to the contrary. He is cursed that mocketh his father, and his heart smote him who did but cut off the skirt of his king's garment, though his enemy; what a monster then is he that kills either! But oh, what a monster, what a devil is that which destroyeth, as far as it is able, the good, the gracious, the great, the glorious, the incomparable God! Truly, sin is such a monster, such a devil, that were its power equal to its spite, and its strength answerable to its malice, the living God should not live a moment.

Omne peccatum est Deicidium, all sin is God-murder: the sinner hates God, Rom. 1:30, and hatred ever wisheth, and, as it is able, worketh the destruction of its object. 'The fool hath said in his heart, There is no God,' Ps. 14:1, i.e., it is a pleasing thought to him, to suppose there were no God; as to guilty prisoners, to imagine there were no judge to arraign and condemn them; whom we fear as hurtful to us, we hate, and wish he were taken out of the way. In order hereunto the sinner strives with God, and contendeth with him, Job 34:7; fighteth against him, Acts 5:39. 'He stretcheth out his hand against God, and strengtheneth himself against the Almighty;' he puts forth all his force, and venteth all his strength; 'he runneth upon him, even on his neck, upon the thick bosses of his bucklers;' runs upon him as one enemy upon another, furiously, without fear, and, as he is able, gets him down, sets his feet on his neck, trampleth on him, and crusheth him, Job 15:25, 26.

Oh how odious, how loathsome, how abominable is sin, that breaks the law, slights the authority, dishonours the name, and to its utmost dethrones and destroys the being of this incomparable God, this self-sufficient, independent, absolutely perfect, eternal, incomprehensible, infinite being, which alone deserves the name of being, and to which all other beings are no beings! Reader, should this God of glory appear to thee, as once to Abraham, and shew thee a glimpse of his excellent glory, that is above the heavens; should he discover to thee but a little of that greatness which the heavens and heaven of heavens cannot contain; of that duration which had no beginning, hath no succession, knoweth no ending; of those perfections that admit of no bounds, no limits, that are incapable of the least addition or accession to them, and then should say unto thee, as when he appeared to Saul, 'Saul, Saul, why percutest thou me?' Man, man, why despisest thou my commands? Why despisest thou my authority? Sinner, how darest thou dishonour my name, and seek my destruction?—what wouldst thou then think of sin? Oh, what wouldst thou then think of thyself for thy sins? Shouldst thou not have other thoughts of sin, and of thyself for sin, than ever yet thou hast had? Wouldst thou not even loathe thyself for being so base, so vile, so unworthy, yea, so mad as to offend and affront, and fight against such a God? Wouldst thou not cry out as Job, 'I have sinned against thee, and what shall I do unto thee, O thou preserver of men?' Job 7:20. I have sinned against thee, an incomparable, infinite, inconceivable being: I have wronged thee, the most high, most holy, most blessed God, and what shall I do unto thee? What amends shall I make thee? What reparation shall I give thee? It is impossible for me, should I weep and wail, and lament and grieve millions of ages, to make the least satisfaction for the injury I have done to such a majesty. Or wouldst thou not say as he in another place, 'Lord, I have heard of thee by the hearing of the ear, but now mine eyes see thee; wherefore I abhor myself, and repent in dust and ashes,' Job 42:5, 6. Lord, I have heard of thee somewhat by thy word, and by thy works, they have told me somewhat of thy beauty and glory, and excellency; howbeit I believed them not, but now mine eyes have seen thy majesty, and royalty, and sovereignty, wherefore I abhor myself, that ever I should transgress thy godly will, that ever I should blaspheme thy great name, that ever I should despise thy supremacy, and fight against thy majesty. Ah, I reprobate turn away mine eyes from myself, cannot endure to behold myself; my stomach is turned against myself, I loathe myself, that ever I should presume and dare to contest and contend with, to wrong and injure thine excellency; I recant all that I have been, all that I have done against thee, and repent, am unfeignedly grieved for it, heartily wish I had never been so, never done so; but since what is past cannot be recalled, I will as far as I can be revenged on myself, for my impudency and distraction, I will lie in the dust, lick the dust, own myself to be much baser and viler than the dust, I will abhor myself in dust and ashes.

This, this is the venom, the malignity of sin, that it is opposite and contrary, offensive and injurious to the incomparable God. This is the consideration which should humble us most for our sins. This was the weight that pressed David down most, and laid him so low in the day of his repentance: 'Against thee, thee only have I sinned, and done evil in thy sight,' Ps. 51:4. Though he had sinned against the enemies of God, in occasioning their blasphemies; against the friends of God, in grieving their spirits; against his whole kingdom, in provoking God to plague them; though he had sinned against Bathsheba, in defiling her body and soul; against Uriah, both in the matter of his wife and life, and against his own body and soul; yet he looks upon these, though great in themselves, yet little, nothing comparatively; the head of the arrow that pierced his heart, was this, 'I have sinned against the Lord,' 2 Sam. 12:13. 'Against thee, thee only have I sinned.' The injury which he did to himself and others, was so inconsiderable, in comparison of the injury he did to God, that he passeth it quite by, in his penitential psalm, and sticks wholly upon this, 'Against thee, thee only have I sinned.'

This is the strongest, the weightiest argument to drive and dissuade from sin; none is like it. When Moses would couch all arguments in one, he useth this instead of all: Num. 32:23, 'But if ye will not do so'—i.e., perform your promise to assist your brethren, till they have conquered their enemies, and are settled in their possessions, what then? What great harm if they do not? Is it not that they sin against their brethren, and wrong their own souls? No, but behold, mark it, it is worthy your attention, and most serious consideration—'ye have sinned against the Lord,' the great, the mighty, the almighty, the incomparable God.

XIX

IF GOD BE INCOMPARABLE, HOW GREAT IS THE MADNESS AND MISERY OF IMPENITENT SINNERS!

2. Secondly, If God be such an incomparable God, it informeth us of the (1). madness and (2). misery of sinners.

i. Of their madness in daring to offend him, and to contend with him. ii. In wilfully losing this incomparable God.

i. How great is their madness in daring to offend him, yea, in daring him to his face! Reader, if thou shouldst see a man without any cause striving with a whole army, hacking and hewing, and provoking them to kill him, you would think, Surely the man is mad, otherwise he would never thus wilfully run himself into a certain ruin. I tell thee every time thou wilfully breakest his laws, thou actest more like a distracted man; for thou fightest against that God who is stronger than millions of armies, who is almighty, and thou provokest him to destroy thee who can wink thee into the other world, and look thee into the eternal lake, and hiss thee into hell-flames. Man, art thou God's match, that thou offerest to enter the list with him? 'Do ye,' saith the apostle, 'provoke the Lord to anger? Are ye stronger than he?' 1 Cor. 10:22. It is one thing to provoke men to anger, and another thing to provoke the Lord to anger. Man hath but a little heart, and a small hand; his anger and power cannot at utmost exceed finite; but God's heart and hand, his anger and power, are both infinite. If the wrath of a king be a messenger of death, what, thinkest thou, is the wrath of immensity, and the stroke of omnipotency? What then is the wrath of a God? Sinner, dost thou know what thou doest when thou breakest his laws, slightest his love, dishonourest his name, grievest his Spirit? I tell thee thou provokest a God who is incomparable in holiness, and hath threatened thy destruction; who is incomparable in power, and can accomplish what he hath threatened; and who is incomparable in truth, and cannot but make good with his arm what he hath spoken with his mouth: 'Woe be to him that striveth with his Maker: let the potsherds strive with the potsherds of the earth,' Isa. 45:1.

God is a God of peace, he hates strife; but if men will be striving, he wisheth them rather to meddle with those that are their matches, poor silly worms like themselves, and not to strive with their Maker, who is infinitely their superior in authority and power, and every perfection. Here is sauciness indeed, for a pitiful nothing to challenge almightiness to battle. 'Who' in his wits, in his senses, that were not quite distracted, 'would set briars and thorns against me in battle? I would go through them, I would burn them up all together,' Isa. 27:4. Briars and thorns are not match to a fire; how easily, how speedily, how certainly doth the fire consume them as soon as it layeth hold of them! How much less is weak man a match for God, who is a consuming fire! When the Roman poet was desired to make verses against his emperor, he answered, *Nolo in eum scribere qui potest proscribere*,[32] I will not jeer and jest with him that can kill me in earnest.

Our Saviour tells us, 'What king going to war against another, sitteth not down first, and consulteth whether he be able with ten thousand to meet him that cometh against him with twenty thousand? Or else while the other is a great way off sendeth to him ambassadors, and desireth conditions of peace?' Luke 14:31, 32. Oh that when the devil and flesh entice the sinner to sport with and make a mock of sin, Prov. 10:23, he would but consider, it is ill jesting with edged tools, it is ill jesting with unquenchable burnings; for how 'can his heart endure or his hands be strong in the day that the great God shall deal with him?' Ezek. 22:14.

ii. Again, How great is their madness who will venture the eternal loss of his God, this incomparable God, forevery base lust! What a madman is he who will stake a million against a mite, a crown against a crumb, substance against shadows, all things against nothing, the blessed boundless God against a moment's sensual delight! Was not Shimei bereft of his wits, to hazard his life for a little uncertain worldly profit by his servant? The Lord Jesus doth most fitly call him a fool, who would hazard and lose the incomparable God for a little corruptible gold, Luke 12:20. The Spirit of God speaks the prodigal to be beside himself, when he left bread, bread enough, bread enough in his father's house, for husks, and not a bellyful neither, and among swine, Luke 15:18–20; and when he came to himself he considered what a madman he was, to wallow among swine, and feed on such brutish fare, which could never fill his belly, when he might have been feasting among the children of God in his Father's house, with plenty of what is bread indeed, able to satisfy a capacious heaven-born soul. Friend, think of

---

[32] "I do not desire to write about him who is able to punish."

it seriously the next time thou art tempted to sin, will this oath, or this cup, or this theft, or this wantonness, or this neglect of duty, balance the everlasting loss of the incomparable God? Will this lust, this moment's pleasure, make amends for the loss of him who is eternal life, and a river of unconceivable and unchangeable pleasures? Shall I be so besotted, bewitched, distracted, as to lose real mercies for lying vanities, the fountain of living waters for broken cisterns, the food of angels for the world's scraps, a precious soul, an inestimable Saviour, an incomparable God, for a toy, a trifle, a poor empty gilded nothing? Did ever any in Bedlam buy so dear, or sell so cheap, or manifest the like madness?

(2). Of the misery of sinners. They shall lose this incomparable God forever; nay, they must have him for their everlasting enemy.

i. Their misery consisteth partly in this, that they must depart forever from this incomparable God: Mat. 7:23, 'Depart from me, ye workers of iniquity;' Mat. 25:41, 'Depart from me, ye cursed.' Oh how dreadful a sound will the word depart make in the sinner's ears; yea, what a deep wound will it make in his heart! Depart from me. Ah! whither do they go that go from God? To depart from riches and honours, and carnal comforts forever, will affect and afflict him to purpose who placeth his happiness in them; to lose health, and liberty, and friends, and relations forever, is no inconsiderable loss to him that knoweth not where to have them made up. To lose the ordinances of God, seasons of grace, the tenders, entreaties, invitations of the gospel forever, is such a loss that a sensualist is incapable of conceiving the greatness of. To lose the communion of perfect spirits, the company of glorious angels, the blessed exercises of the heavenly host forever, will not a little affright and amaze and vex and terrify the wicked, when they once come to have their eyes opened, and their consciences awakened in the other world. But to depart from the incomparable God forever, to lose the only paradise of pleasures, the only fountain of living waters, the only author of true felicity; to lose the unsearchable mine of riches, the inexhaustible well of salvation, the inestimable Sun of righteousness; to lose the dearest father, the wisest guide, the strongest shield, the sweetest love, the closest friend, the tenderest mercy, the richest grace, the highest honour, the only happiness; to lose the Lord of life, the Lord of glory, the Lord of lords; to lose the God of hope, the God of all grace, the God of all consolation, the God of peace, the God of gods, the God and Father of our Lord Jesus Christ, the incomparable God; and to lose him totally and forever, is the loss of all losses, is such a loss as no tongue can declare, no mind can conceive, is such a loss as never was the like before it, nor shall, nor can be the like after it. He that hath lost God, hath nothing left that is good, he hath lost all that was worth having or saving: 'Lord, whither shall we go if we go from thee? Thou hast the words of eternal life,' John 6:68.

Reader, how great is the sinner's loss in the other world, how great soever his gain is in this! Ah! 'Where is his hope, though he hath gained, when God shall take away his soul?' Job 27:8. Can the greatest gain counterbalance the loss of him to whom the whole world, yea, millions of worlds, are trash and trifles?

The greatness of any loss is to be measured by the excellency and value of that which we lose; therefore if God be so incomparable in all perfections, the loss of sinners, who lose this God totally and eternally, must be an incomparable loss. As there is no gain equal to the gain of a God, all other gains are but painted baubles or butterflies to this; so there is no loss equal to the loss of a God, all other losses are but bugbears to fright children with to this; this is a loss with a witness, a loss which nothing can countervail, supply, or make up, in which all that is good is gone forever. As Micah said to the Israelites, when they asked him what he ailed to cry out so, 'Ye have taken away my god, and what have I more?' Judges 18:22. So will the sinner in the other world screech horribly, and complain heavily of his deceitful flesh, which now he makes such provision for, Thou hast taken away my God, and what have I more? I am poor, a beggar, nothing worth, worse than nought, wholly ruined, utterly undone by thee, I have lost my God, and with him all that is good.

Reader, if thou livest without God, ponder, oh ponder in the midst of all thy gettings, what thou art losing, yea, what thou shalt lose, if thou dost not return, forever and ever. Did the disciples weep and wail, that they should see the face of a good man no more on earth: 'Sorrowing most of all, for the words that he spake unto them, that they should see his face no more'? Acts 20:38. And dost thou think it will not fill thy heart with sorrow, and cut it with anguish, to hear the blessed God, the incomparable God, say to thee, Sinner, farewell, farewell forever, thou shalt see my face no more forever! Believe it, those words will sound more dolefully in thine ears than thou art now aware of; they will be a passing bell to all thy hopes, and joys, and comforts, and delights; they will be a knell to toll the death and burial of whatsoever may be refreshing and reviving to thee, of all thine ease, and rest, and liberty, and peace, and health, and strength, and friends, and relations, and all that may in the least conduce to thy comfort or happiness.

Now possibly thou canst be merry enough without God; thou hadst rather have his room than his company, preferrest a life without him before a life with him; and sayest unto him, 'Depart from me, I desire not the knowledge of thy ways,' Job 21:14. And the reason of this atheism and profaneness, is thine ignorance; thou knowest not what a fountain of life, what bowels of love, what a hive of sweetness, what an ocean of happiness the blessed incomparable God is, neither believest what Scripture speaks hereof; but when once thou enterest into the other world, and hast lost this God irrecoverably, thou shalt know what thou hast lost; but then, if ever, that saying of the wise man will be verified, 'He that increaseth knowledge, increaseth sorrow,' Eccles. 1:18. And then thou shalt believe the truth of the glass of Scripture in its representations of the beautiful face of God, though thy faith will be the faith of a devil, to thy terror and torment. Ah, sinner, when thou shalt know and believe what a vast treasure, what a river of pleasure, what a perfect good, what fulness of joy, what solid comfort, what real satisfaction, what a weight of glory thou hast lost forever, without the least hopes and possibility of regaining, and lost for base, vile, sordid lusts, for a little foolish brutish momentary pleasure; what thoughts, thinkest thou, will then seize thee? What anguish and remorse surprise thee? Ah, how wilt thou loathe and hate, and curse thyself for thy folly and madness! Thou wilt gnash thy teeth for envy at them that sit at heaven's table, feasting with the fruit of the tree of life, and drinking of the pure rivers of water which flow from the throne of God and the Lamb: and thou wilt weep and wail for thy own distraction, that thou shouldst refuse the offers of all those dainties, and delicates, and delights, when they were made to thee in the day of thy life; that thou shouldst shut thy own mouth, and wilfully refuse all those rich and costly cordials, and shut the door of heaven and happiness against thee with thine own hands. Ah, sinner, little dost thou know at the present what it is to lose this God. Other losses may be corrective, but this is destructive; God whips in others, but he executes in this; other losses may be the part of his children, but this is the portion of devils. All joy, all comfort, is stabbed to the heart, pierced through, the heard-blood of it is let out with this one word, sharper than any two-edged sword, Depart: 'Write this man comfortless,' (as it was said of one, Jer. 22:30,) 'a man that shall not prosper all his days.' Write this poor soul comfortless, a soul that shall not have a bit of bread, a drop of water, a glimpse of light, a moment's ease, a

crumb of comfort, all the long day of eternity. Ah, friend, think of it be-
times: 'Woe be to thee if God depart from thee,' Hosea 9:12.

ii. Their misery consisteth in this also, that they shall have this incomparable God for their enemy. As there is no friend like God, and therefore
their privative misery must be great, exceeding great, inconceivably great;
so there is no enemy like God; and therefore the positive misery of sinners
must be matchless and beyond all comparisons. The greater any one's
power and anger are, the greater their misery is who fall under the stroke
of that power and the force of that anger. God is incomparable in power; he
worketh arbitrarily, irresistibly, omnipotently; he hath a mighty and an almighty arm. God is incomparable in anger; his anger roots up, pulls down,
kills, makes horrid slaughters, removeth the mountains, shaketh the foundations of the earth, is a consuming fire, burning and wasting all that comes
near it. 'Thou, even thou, art to be feared; for none may stand when thou
art angry,' Ps. 76:7. Woe, therefore, to them that have this God for their
enemy; 'It is a fearful thing to fall into the hands of the living God,' Heb.
10:31. David chose rather to fall into the hands of God than men, 2 Sam.
24:14, because he was a child of God, though afflicted sharply by him; for
love can consist with anger, though not with hatred; and therefore desired,
since he must be scourged, to be whipped by a loving Father, who would
consider his strength, what he could bear, as well as his fault and offence,
and accordingly use his rod, rather than by a cruel enemy, who hated him,
and had not the least mercy or pity for him. Beside, this world is the stage
whereon the mercy of God acteth its part. Justice must have its course and
solemn triumph in the other world. He is here good to all; his sun shineth,
and rain falleth upon the just and unjust, Ps. 145:9; Mat. 5:45. Therefore, it
is better for any man upon earth to fall into the hands of God than the best
friend or nearest relation in the world. But the sinner is the object only of
God's wrath, of his hatred, of his abhorrency, after death. God then puts off
all pity, all tenderness, all bowels towards him; and the other world is the
place wherein his justice, that is now clouded and eclipsed, shall shine forth
in its full force and strength, and appear in all its beauty and brightness.
And, therefore, it must of necessity be a fearful thing for a poor creature to
fall into the hands of the living God; to have nothing but his naked flesh,
his own weak soul, to bear the stroke of infinite power, set on and urged to
strike home by infinite anger, and that forever.

All the rackings and torturings, the extreme pains and aches, the violent convulsions and consternations, the dreadful horror and anguish, the
everlasting chains of darkness, the never-dying worm, and the fire that

never goeth out, of the devils and damned, are but the expressions and fruits of the matchless power and anger of this incomparable God. Therefore they are called wrath, Rom. 2:5; the wrath of God, John 3:36; and wrath to come, 1 Thes. 1:10. Reader, think of it; if the wrath of a king, a man like thyself, though clothed with more civil power and strength, be as 'the roaring of a lion,' Prov. 19:12, which makes all the beasts of the forest to quake and tremble, Amos 3:6, what then is the wrath of an almighty, infinite God? If he wound his friends, the objects of his eternal choice, the travail of his beloved Son's soul, those on whom he intendeth to glorify the riches of his love and grace forever, in the day of his anger for their disobedience, with the wound of an enemy, yea, with the wounds of a cruel one, Jer. 30:14; if he break their bones, and cause the arrow of his quiver to enter into their reins; if he fill their souls with bitterness, and make them drunk with wormwood; if he makes them water their couches with tears, and go mourning all the day long; if his anger causeth them to roar incessantly, and his terrors make them distracted; if he be to them as a bear lying in wait, and as a lion in secret places;—how will he wound thee, his enemy? How will he deal with thee whom he infinitely hateth? What a bear, what a lion, what a fire will he be to thee! How unable wilt thou be to stand under, and yet how impossible to avoid the weight of his omnipotent arm and infinite anger! Lay it to heart timely, and make thy peace with him through his Son, that thou mayest prevent it. Sure I am thou wouldest not fry in flames, or boil alive in a furnace of scalding lead a thousand years, for this whole world's command ten thousand years. Ah, why then shouldst thou, for a little profit, a little pleasure, a little honour for a few days,—for thy life is but a vapour,— bring thyself under a necessity of frying in the flames, and boiling in the furnace of the Almighty God's anger forever and ever? O friend, be wise on this side the other world.

XX

IF GOD BE INCOMPARABLE, HOW MONSTROUS IS THEIR PRIDE WHO COMPARE THEMSELVES TO THE INCOMPARABLE GOD!

3. Thirdly, If God be such an incomparable God, it informeth us what abominable pride and desperate presumption they are guilty of who compare with and prefer themselves before this God. If he be so transcendently excellent in his being, attributes, word, and works, how desperately saucy and impudent are they who put themselves in the balance with God! 'Behold, all nations to me are as nothing, yea, less than nothing, and vanity. To whom then will ye liken me? Or to what will ye compare me?' Isa. 40:17, 18. To liken God to any is the grossest idolatry, and to liken any to God is the highest arrogancy. Babylon, that sets herself in the throne of God, and exalteth herself above all that is called God, is the mystery of iniquity, the man of sin, in truth, the dregs of the very devil, 2 Thes. 2:9. It is a debasing God, not to adore him, and admire him according to his excellent majesty and vast immensity; what a debasing then is it of God to compare him to poor pitiful nothings, as all men and angels are to him! He debaseth himself to open his eyes upon men, upon angels, to behold things that are done in heaven and earth, Ps. 113:5. But he will not debase himself to compare with men and angels; he scorneth to put himself into the scales with them; he is infinitely above and beyond all comparatives, all superlatives. Comparisons, we say, are odious; but no comparison that ever was hath in the least degree that odiousness which this hath, for a man or an angel to compare with their Maker. The slime, and clay, and earth may very much better compare with the potter; both are narrow, limited beings; both are earth and clay; yet the potter would think it a great dishonour to him, who hath a body curiously wrought, and a heaven-born spiritual immortal soul, and desperate arrogancy in the clay and dirt which he trampleth on, to compare with him. And is it not greater pride in man to compare with God,

when there is an infinite distance between them in all things? Yet so ambitious and arrogant is man that he dares to do this. Angels and Adam both aspired to equal their Maker; they would needs be independent and self-sufficient; they endeavoured to cut off the entail, and to hold wholly and only of themselves; but they ruined themselves, and made themselves baser than beasts, by aspiring thus to raise themselves to that impossible pitch of a partnership with God.

It is a favour that men and angels may be like God in some rays and beams of his holiness and purity; but it is impossible for men or angels to be like God in the rich jewels of his crown, his independency, absolute perfection, self-sufficiency, infiniteness, and supremacy. He stamped some impressions of himself upon his creatures, but he took no impressions of his creatures upon himself; if they were made in his likeness, he was not made in their likeness; it is devilish impudency and blasphemy for the highest creature to weigh with the Creator. This was Lucifer's pride, 'I will ascend into heaven, I will exalt my throne above the stars, I will be like the most High,' Isa. 14:13, 14. But his pride got a fall, and a shrewd one too. God cannot brook a rival, he cannot bear an equal, there must be but one sun in the heavens. A prince may take it kindly from his subjects if they endeavour to imitate him in his mercy, justice, temperance, chastity, and in those things that are general and common to him and them, because hereby his subjects honour him, for by their imitation of him they acknowledge excellency in him; but if his subjects shall undertake to imitate him in his regalia, those things that are proper to him as a king—should they aspire to make laws, to make peace and war, to wear the crown, sway the sceptre, and ascend the throne, he could not bear it, but would judge them rebels guilty of high treason and worthy of death, because hereby they extremely dishonour him, viz., in making themselves equal to him, and robbing him of that superiority which God hath given him. So God is pleased and delighted that men and angels should resemble him in those perfections of his that are common and communicable, as to be patient, and meek, and loving, and righteous, and heavenly, and holy, because hereby they glorify him, Mat. 5:16. But if the creatures should go about to be like him in the peculiar cognisances of the deity, his self-sufficiency, independency, governing others at their will, enacting laws to oblige the consciences of others, exacting worship from their fellow-creatures; so God cannot, God will not suffer it, for hereby they go about to rob him of his supremacy, to dethrone and un-god him. How often doth God tell us in Scripture to quell such presumptu-ous thoughts, that he is not man's fellow, man's familiar: 'God is not a man,' Num. 23:19. 'I am God, and not man,' Hosea 11:9. 'He is not a man as I am,' saith Job, chap. 9:32. Though God was pleased out of his infinite grace to become man, that man might once more be like God in those communica-ble properties forementioned, yet he will not permit it, nay, it is altogether impossible for man to become God, and be like him in the special preroga-tives of the deity. There is still an infinite distance between the divine and the human nature. They who prate of being godded, and turned into the essence of the deity, as some have impudently and blasphemously written, are either intolerably weak or devilishly wicked, or both. Now, because many are guilty of the strange presumption to compare with God who little think it, I shall very briefly name two or three sorts of men.

(1). Such as quarrel with the precepts of God, as if they were too strict, too precise, too pure, and that God commanded more than was needful, Ps. 2:2; Rom. 8:7. This is a comparing with God, yea, a preferring ourselves be-fore God; and such speak as if they would be in God's throne to make laws, and as if they would enact better laws, more conducing to and convenient for the welfare of mankind. Because man hath vitiated his nature and dis-tempered all his faculties, he is angry at God for enjoining him a strict diet, and forbidding him what would feed his disease. A foul stomach loatheth the wholesomest food.

(2). When men question the providences of God, as if they were not good, and wise, and righteous, these compare, yea, prefer themselves be-fore God; their voice is like Absalom's: Oh that I were judge! Things should not go thus at six and sevens; see here is none to do justice to you. Oh that I governed the world! There should be no such disorders as are now, no such inequality amongst men. The righteous should not perish, nor the wicked flourish as they do. These ways are not equal, Ezek. 33:17, 20. These men contend with God for sovereignty: 'Why strivest thou with him?' Job 33:13. These men accuse God of folly, and think themselves wiser; 'but shall he that contendeth with God instruct him?' Job 40:2. He that complains of God's dealings undertakes to teach God in what manner and by what means the world should be better governed. These men compare with God for jus-tice, nay, condemn him of injustice: Job 40:8, 'Wilt thou condemn me, that thou mayest be righteous?'

God's ways are often secret; his paths are in the seas, and his goings in deep waters, Ps. 77:19; and because men cannot fathom them, therefore they find fault with them. He writes his mind often in shorthand, in dark characters, and because poor blind man cannot read them, therefore he wrangleth with them: 'Thy judgments are a great deep,' Ps. 36:6.

(3). When men tax the decrees of God, as if they were unrighteous, partial, and ordered with respect of persons, they then compare with God, as if, in case they had been at heaven's council-table when all things were debated and concluded, there should have been more mild and moderate, more just and righteous resolves and conclusions. These men think and speak evil of the things they understand not; and it would become them better to mind faith and repentance, and ensure their effectual calling, than pry into or meddle with those secrets of heaven. No man hath a line long enough to measure God by; his eternal works and ways are beyond all our understandings and apprehensions, and so much fitter for our admiration than curious disquisition, Rom. 9:17–24.

(4). Once more: those princes, or masters, or parents, which command what God forbids, or forbid what God commands, compare with God and usurp his authority; for their power to command, and right to be obeyed, must, in their conceits, be equal to God's, or else why do they give laws in opposition to his? Or how can they expect to be obeyed? They who command divine worship to bread and wine, and places, or any creature, compare with and prefer themselves before God, which is desperate pride and presumption, 1 Kings 21:9–11; 2 Sam. 13:28.

XXI

IF GOD BE INCOMPARABLE, THEN INCOMPARABLE SERVICE AND WORSHIP IS DUE TO HIM

4. Fourthly, If God be an incomparable God, then incomparable service and worship is due to him. All service must be suitable to its object. The higher the prince, the higher honour he doth and may expect. The heathen were sensible of this, that such worship must be given to their deities as was suitable to them; therefore the Persians, who worshipped the sun, offered to him a flying horse, noting strength and swiftness, because the sun was strong to run his race. God is a great God, and therefore must have great worship. Solomon gives this reason why the temple, the place of God's worship, must be great; 2 Chron. 2:5, the house which I build is great; why? For great is our God above all gods. A great palace is most suitable and becoming a great prince. It reflects upon God, it is a slighting him, to give him anything that is ordinary, as it is to a king to be put off with common entertainment at the houses of his subjects. As he is the best, so he will be served with the best. 'Cursed be the deceiver who hath in his flock a male, and offereth to the Lord a corrupt thing.' Why, what is the matter, that there must be such care about, and choice of his sacrifices? God himself gives you the reason, and a good reason for it: 'For I am a great King, saith the Lord of hosts, and my name is dreadful among the heathen,' Mal. 1:14. Petty princes may be owned and served with petty presents; but a great king, a great sovereign, must have great sacrifices.

When the prophet had described the incomparable excellency of God, how all nations were to him as the least drop in a bucket to the ocean, and the small dust in the balance to the whole earth, as nothing and less than nothing, he presently infers, 'Lebanon is not sufficient to burn, nor all the beasts thereof for a burnt-offering,' Isa. 40:15-17. Lebanon abounded in all spices for incense and perfumes, and in cattle for sacrifices and burnt offerings; but all the spices and perfumes there, all the beasts and cattle there, were below and insufficient for so incomparable a being; he is so great that no service can be great enough for him.

(1). This incomparable God calls for incomparable awe and reverence. Excellency commandeth awe. 'Should not his excellency make you afraid, and his dread fall upon you?' Job 13:11. Should not the vastness of his perfections provoke you to awfulness in your conversations? 'His name alone is excellent,' Ps. 148:13. The greater distance between any persons, the greater reverence is expected. The husband is the head of the wife, therefore she is commanded to reverence her husband, 1 Cor. 7; Eph. 5:33. There is a great civil distance between masters and servants, therefore the command runs: 'Servants be obedient to your masters with fear and trembling,' Eph. 6:5. But now between God and us there is an infinite distance, and therefore there ought to be, if it were possible, infinite reverence; he is so vastly above and beyond all others in excellency, that he alone deserves the name of excellency, therefore his name is holy and reverend, Ps. 111:9, and he is to be greatly feared. The greatest excellency calleth for the greatest reverence. 'Great is the Lord, and greatly to be praised, he is to be feared above all gods,' Ps. 96:4. This use David makes of God's incomparableness: 'Who in the heavens can be compared to the Lord? Who among the sons of the mighty can be likened to the Lord?' what then; what followeth on this? 'God is greatly to be feared in the assembly of his saints, and to be had in reverence of all them that are round about him,' Ps. 89:6, 7; because in our whole conversations we must walk with God, therefore we are commanded 'to be in the fear of the Lord all the day long,' Prov. 23:17. But because in ordinances we have more immediately and specially to do with him—then we are said to appear before him, Ps. 42:2—therefore we are bound therein to be most awful and reverential. Subjects shew most reverence in the presence-chamber of their sovereign. Oh with what awe and dread should mortals appear in the presence of him who inhabiteth eternity! Should dust and ashes draw nigh to the mighty possessor of heaven and earth? Eccles. 5:1, 2, 'Keep thy foot when thou goest to the house of God, and be more ready to hear than to give the sacrifice of fools; be not rash with thy mouth, let not thine heart be hasty to utter anything before God;' but why all this care and caution? 'For God is in heaven, and thou art on earth.' His incomparable majesty calleth for incomparable reverence: majesty is dreadful. He is clothed with majesty, Ps. 93:1, all over majesty, therefore let all the earth stand in awe of him. He is adorned, surrounded with majesty, therefore we must be filled with the awe of him. Isa. 2:10, 19, 20, fear and majesty are three times conjoined. His incomparable power calls for incomparable reverence. Power is awful; and the greater the power is, the greater awe is required. Mat. 10:28, 'Fear not them that can kill the body, and can do no more; but fear him who is able to cast soul and body into hell.' As if Christ had said, I know you are of timorous spirits, and men of fearful tempers; ye are apt to tremble, and to be frightened at everything; well, I will direct you how you may make this passion advantageous to you—viz., by turning the stream into its proper channel, by placing your fear on its proper object; I will tell you of one worthy of your fear, who deserveth to be feared: so, Luke 12:4, 5, 'I will forewarn you whom ye shall fear,' I will offer you an object meet for your fear, 'Fear him who, after he hath killed, hath power to cast into hell; yea, I say unto you, Fear him.' You are apt, like children, to be frightened with bugbears, and to dread them that can only raze the skin and pinch the flesh, and at the most can but take from you a life that will fall of itself within a few days; well, I will advise you whom to stand in awe of: Fear him that can kill you and damn you, that can send your bodies to the grave, and your souls to unquenchable flames; yea, I say unto you, Fear him.

(2). This incomparable God calls for incomparable humility and lowliness of spirit from us. The height of God must lay man low, and the matchless excellency of God make him base in his own eyes. When we behold ourselves in the glass of those that have little or nothing that is good or praiseworthy, or that have less than ourselves, then we spread out our plumes, and are puffed up with pride, and judge ourselves comely creatures; but if we would behold ourselves in the glass of the incomparable God, in whose sight the heavens are unclean, in whose presence angels vail their faces, to whom ten thousand suns are perfect darkness, and all the world less than nothing; how should we pluck in our plumes, and abhor ourselves for our pride! Man never comes to a right knowledge of himself, what a pitiful, abominable wretch he is, till he comes to a right knowledge of God, what an excellent incomparable majesty he is. As when men stand high, and look downward on those below them, that are meaner and viler than themselves, their heads are giddy, and swim with conceitedness, they then are somebody in their own opinions; but when they look upwards to the great God, the sun, the soul, the substance of all worth and excellency, that meagrim[33] or high-mindedness is prevented. The best men upon a sight of God, the incomparable God, though the more excellent he is, the more cause they have of joy in having so rich a portion, yet instead of loving, have loathed themselves, and instead of admiring, have abhorred themselves. When Isaiah saw the God of glory sitting on his throne in his brightness and beauty, encircled with millions of celestial courtiers covering their faces, as ashamed of their drops in the presence of the ocean, and crying, Holy, holy, holy, as apprehending his purity beyond all their expressions, and his perfections exceeding all their apprehensions, what thoughts had he of himself? Oh what a poor, pitiful, contemptible creature did he think himself; yea, what an uncomely, loathsome, abominable creature was he in his own eye! 'Woe to me,' saith he, 'I am undone, I am a man of unclean lips, for mine eyes have seen the Lord of hosts,' Isa. 6:4, 5.

(3). This incomparable God calls for incomparable love, the top, the cream of our affections. Good is the object of love. *Amor est complacentia boni*,[34] according to the moralists; the greater therefore the good is, the greater love it requireth; and God being the greatest good, must have the greatest love. This is the great and first command, Mat. 22:37; this is, as I may say, the only command, Deut. 10:12; this is all the commands in one, Rom. 13:10. Love is the decalogue contracted, and the decalogue is love opened and explained. 'Thou shalt love the Lord thy God with all thy heart, with all thy soul, with all thy strength, with all thy mind,' Mat. 22:37. God being the greatest perfection, must have the greatest affection.

The greatest love (for God is love, 1 John 4:8) calls for the greatest love. He deserves the greatest extensively, the heart, soul, mind, strength; the greatest intensively, all the heart, all the soul, all the mind, all the strength. Reader, thy love to him must be so great that thy love to thy father, mother, wife, child, house, land, and life, must be hatred in comparison of it, and in competition with it, Luke 16:26. The truth is, there is nothing worthy of our love like God; nay, there is nothing worthy of our love beside God. All our friends, and relations, and estates, and worldly blessings, are nothing lovely, but as they are his creatures, his comforts, instruments for his glory, and as they have relation to him; nay, sabbaths, sacraments, seasons of grace, are no more lovely than as they are his institutes, and means of com-

---

33 Probably from "megrim," meaning "flight or fancy."
34 "Love is the delight of the good."

munion with his majesty. 'I love the habitation of thy house,' (why? Because) 'it is the place where thine honour dwelleth,' Ps. 26:8. Once more; grace itself is not lovely, but as it is the image and conformity unto, the pleasure and delight of, that which fitteth and maketh meet for the love, embraces, and fruition of this incomparable God. Desire and delight are the two acts of love, distinguished only by the absence or presence of the object. When the object beloved is absent, the soul acts towards it in desire. When the object is present, the soul acteth towards it in delight. The former is the motion, the latter the rest and repose of the soul. Now the incomparable God must have incomparable desires, panting, Ps. 42:1, longing, yea, fainting, out of vehemency of desire, Ps. 119:20, 40, 81. God must be desired above all: Ps. 73:25, 'Whom have I in heaven but thee? And there is none upon earth that I desire beside thee.' The incomparable God must have incomparable delight: 'I will go to the altar of God my joy, of God my exceeding joy,' Ps. 43:4. The soul must be ravished, ecstasied in the presence and enjoyment of God, Cant. 2:4.

(4). The incomparable God must have incomparable trust. The more able and faithful any person is, the more firmly we trust him. Now, God is incomparable in power, he hath an almighty arm; incomparable in faithfulness, he cannot lie, Titus 1:2. 'It is impossible for him to lie,' Heb. 6:18. Therefore God must have our surest love and firmest faith, Heb. 6:18; Rom. 4:20. We must esteem his words as good as deeds; and rely on all he promiseth as if it were already performed. We must not stagger or waver, but 'draw nigh to him with full assurance of faith,' Heb. 10:22: His bonds must be looked upon, for they are as good, as ready money; and we must rejoice in hope of the good things promised as if we had them in hand, Rom. 5:2, 3.

(5). This incomparable God must have incomparable obedience in the whole course of our lives. The more virtuous, or gracious, or honourable, or excellent, the person is with whom we walk, the more we weigh our words, and ponder the paths of our feet, and watch over ourselves. God is incomparable in purity, in jealousy, in majesty, in excellency; therefore they who are ever under his eye and in his presence, and who walk with him, must walk, not as they do when with ordinary persons, carelessly and negligently, but circumspectly, accurately, exactly, to a hair's breadth, as on a ridge, ἀκριβῶς,[35] Eph. 5:15. His law must be kept to a tittle, in every punctilio, as the apple of the eye, Prov. 7:2, which is offended with the least mote of dust; and this obedience must be not only at some seasons and in

---

35 "Carefully."

some actions, but always and in all things. 'As he who hath called you is holy, so be ye holy in all manner of conversation,' 1 Pet. 1:15.

All our service to this incomparable God must be incomparable. Little service is unsuitable to a great God, 1 Chron. 29:1, 2. 'David the king said unto all the congregation, Solomon my son, whom alone God hath chosen, is yet young and tender, and the work (i.e., of building the temple) is great; for the palace is not for man, but for the Lord God. Now I have prepared with all my might for the house of my God,' &c.

5. Fifthly, If God be an incomparable God, it informeth us of his infinite grace and condescension, to take so much notice of, and do so much for man. The height of the person that bestoweth a favour, and the meanness and unworthiness of the object on whom it is bestowed, doth exceedingly advance and heighten the grace and goodness of him that doth it. Oh what grace is it then for the most High, the God of heaven, the God whom the heaven of heavens cannot contain, to manifest such, respect to vile, sinful dust and ashes, yea, to them that are rebels and traitors against his majesty, and thereby worthy of hell! David admireth it, and is amazed at it, Ps. 8:1. 'O Lord, our Lord, how excellent is thy name in all the earth! and thy glory is above the heavens.' What followeth? 'What is man that thou art mindful of him, or the son of man that thou visitest him?' That God, the excellent God, the God famous in all the earth, the God glorious above the heavens, should mind man, poor, silly, simple man—weak, frail, dying man—sinful, filthy, polluted man—lost, wretched, miserable man, could not but affect the heart of David with admiration and astonishment. 'What is man that thou art mindful of him?' He is altogether below thy thoughts, and unworthy to be a moment in thy mind: 'Or the son of man that thou visitest him?' He doth not deserve to be visited by the beasts of the earth, much less to be visited by the angels of heaven, and least of all by the God of heaven. He may well say as the centurion, 'Lord, I am unworthy that thou shouldst come under my roof, neither thought I myself worthy to come unto thee,' Mat. 8:8. David wonders that God should mind man so much as to make the heavens, and those glorious lamps there, for his use and comfort: 'When I consider the heavens, the work of thy fingers, the moon and the stars which thou hast made; what is man that thou art mindful of him?' But how much more cause had he to wonder that the heaven of heavens, the God of heaven, the Sun of righteousness, the light of lights, should do so much, and be so much himself for the good and comfort of man!

God doth manifest much grace and condescension in taking such care of men's bodies and outward concerns. You would think it a great grace and condescension in a king to take care night and day of a poor beggar, to see to it himself, and not to leave it to servants or any others, that he have food, and raiment, and liberty, and peace, and safety every day, that his bed be made well and easy for him every night—that when he is sick he have physic, and cordials, and tendance, and should constantly visit him himself in person, that in all his wants he be supplied, in all his weaknesses supported, in all his dangers defended, and in all his distresses delivered; if this king should never stir from this beggar, but do all this in his own person; if he himself should spread his table, and provide his food, and be at the sole charge of his garments, and put them on, and make his bed, and stand by him all night while he slept, to prevent any evil that might befall him, and go up and down with him all day to protect him and counsel him, and relieve him, as occasion required, you would be amazed at the favour and kindness and condescension of this prince. Believe it, reader—surely seeing is believing —the King of kings, and Lord of lords, he whose name is 'I am,' he to whom all the kings and princes and potentates of the world are dross and dirt and dung, the incomparable God doth more than all this, very much more for thee every day and every night, and that in his own person. He sendeth thee all thy bread, and drink, and clothes, and makes them refreshing to thee. He provides thy habitation and lodging, and commandeth sleep for thee. He is with thee continually in all thy outgoings, incomings, to preserve thee alive, to enable thee to thy motions, to succeed thy lawful undertakings, to relieve thee in thy necessities, and to defend thee from all thine adversaries. And is not this condescension worthy of all admiration? Oh what grace is it, that the incomparable God, who hath millions of glorious angels waiting on him, and ten thousand times ten thousand always ministering to him, should thus wait on, and watch over poor crawling worms, night and day for good, Acts 7:2; Job 7:20; Ps. 4:8; Hosea 2:8; Gen. 32:9–11; Ps. 34:3–5; Heb. 1:3; Ps. 145:5, 7. Job wonders that God should condescend to correct man for his faults: 'What is man, that thou dost magnify him? That thou settest thine heart upon him, that thou visitest him every morning?' &c., Job 7:17, 18. How much then doth God condescend, to be his constant guide and guard, to keep him night and day lest any hurt him? Oh the grace of this God! This incomparable God doth much more magnify his grace and condescension in the care he is pleased to take of men's precious souls. Herein he sheweth the riches of his mercy, the exceeding abundant riches of his grace, Eph. 2:5, 7. Reader, is it not condescending grace in the highest degree, nay, beyond all degrees, for this selfsufficient, absolutely perfect, incomparable God, when the soul of man lay naked, starving, restless, encompassed with enemies, unpitied of all creatures, weltering in its blood, gasping for breath, ready every moment to fetch its last, and to be seized on by devils, dragged to their dungeon of darkness, there to fry in untolerable flames forever; for him to look on man in this loathsome condition with an eye of favour and love, to clothe it with the righteousness of a God, to feed it with that flesh which is meat indeed, and with that blood which is drink indeed, to give it rest in his own bowels and bosom, to bind up its wounds, and raise it from the dead, and make it free from the slavery of Satan and his bondage to sin and death and hell, and to adopt it for his own child, accept it as perfectly righteous, marry it to his only-begotten, the heir of all things, dwell in it by his own blessed Spirit, and carry it on eagle's wings, and conduct it safe through the wilderness of the world, and in spite of all the lions and wolves, and serpents and adders, and giants, and Anakims and Canaanites that opposed it, to bring it to a heavenly Canaan, to fulness of joy, and rivers of pleasures, and crowns of life, and weights of glory, there to reign in and with his own incomparable majesty for ages, generations, millions of ages, yea unto all eternity? Friend, friend, what is condescending grace, if this be not? Alas, the incomparable God had no obligation to man, he stood in no way need of man, he is incapable of the least good by man; he would have been as happy as he is at present, if the race of mankind had been ruined and had perished. Besides, he was infinitely disobliged by man, and had all the reason in the world to destroy him; and yet he is pleased to be as studious of man's welfare, and as solicitous about it as if it had been his own. Abigail wondered that David, anointed to a kingdom, should take her to be his wife; she scarce judged herself worthy to wash the feet of his servants, 1 Sam. 25:41. Mayest not thou wonder more that the incomparable God should marry thee to himself, who art unworthy to be his servant? David admired that God should do so much for him. Hast thou not cause to say as he did, Lord, what am I, and what is my father's house, that thou hast brought me up hitherto, pardoned, instructed, renewed me, taken me into thy own family? And yet, as if this were a small thing in thy sight, thou speakest of thy servant's house for a great while to come, thou art pleased to speak of thy servant for an everlasting kingdom of honour and pleasure, 2 Sam. 7:18. And this condescending grace, or gracious condescension, is much the more admirable, if we consider the means by which this great work of man's recovery was effected. The incomparable God that is so great, so high, without all bounds, beyond all understanding, becomes a weak, weary, hungry, contemptible man. Reader, here is amazing condescension. The Lord of all becomes a servant, the Lord of glory becomes of no reputation, the bread of life is hungry, and the only rest is weary, and the prince of life is put to death. This is that which angels pry into with such astonishing pleasure, that God should become man, the lawgiver be made under the law, he that tempteth no man to evil, neither can be tempted to evil, should be violently tempted many days together by all the powers of darkness, the only blessing should be made a curse, that liberty should be in bonds, and truth itself belied, and justice condemned, and heaven be laid in the belly of the earth. This is marvellous grace, indeed, such as passeth all knowledge, Eph. 3:18, 19. If all the glorious cherubims and seraphims, angels and archangels, had condescended to have been turned into toads and serpents, it had not been by the thousandth part so great a condescension, as for the incomparable God to become man; for those heavenly spirits, and toads and serpents, do *convenire in aliquo tertio*,[36] meet in the genus of creatures; there is but a finite difference between the former and the latter. But God and man meet in no third, in no genus; between them there is an infinite distance. There never was, there never shall be, there never can be the like condescension.

---

[36] "Meet in a third place."

XXII

LABOUR FOR ACQUAINTANCE WITH THE INCOMPARABLE GOD: MOTIVES TO IT; THE KNOWLEDGE OF GOD IS SANCTIFYING, SATISFYING, SAVING

II. Secondly, This doctrine may be useful by way of counsel.

1. Study the knowledge of this God, who is so incomparable. We are all ambitious to be acquainted with persons that are eminent and excellent in place, or power, or parts, or piety, and judge it our interest and an honour to us so to be. If we could hear of one as strong as Samson, whom no cords could hold, who could slay hundreds with a jawbone; or of one as old as Methuselah, who could tell us what was done in many centuries of years; or of one as wise as Solomon, who could speak to the nature of all creatures, and answer the hardest questions we could put to him; or of one as holy as Adam in innocency, or the elect angels, who never broke the law of their Maker, but were as pure and perfect as when they came immediately out of his hands; how should we throng, and thrust, and crowd to such men! What pains should we take! What cost should we be at to obtain the favour and honour of their acquaintance! Surely, we should think, we could never view them enough, or value them enough, or know enough of them, or discourse enough with them. But, alas, what are such men, if we could find them in the world, to the blessed God? What motes, what drops, what poor pitiful nothings! What is a strong Samson to the Almighty God, but as straw, as chaff, as rotten wood, as all weakness! What is the age of Methuselah to the duration of the eternal God, to whose age millions of years add not a moment, but as a minute, as nothing! Ps. 39:5. What is the wisdom of Solomon to all the treasures of wisdom and knowledge which are in the only wise God, but a curious web of folly! Col. 2:9. What is the holiness of an angel to the holiness of God, but as a candle to the sun, yea, as perfect night and darkness to the noonday! Oh, therefore, how shouldst thou labour to know

this God! How industrious shouldst thou be to be acquainted with him! When the queen of Sheba had heard of the extraordinary knowledge and abilities of Solomon, she came from the utmost parts of the earth to see his person, and to hear his wisdom. But behold, reader, a greater than Solomon is here. Solomon was an idiot, an innocent, to this object, which I request thee to know: 'The understanding of God is infinite,' Ps. 147:5: 'There is no searching of his understanding,' Isa. 40:28. Indeed, it is bottomless, and therefore can never be found out. His knowledge can never be known fully, no, not by angels themselves. Do men beat their brains, and consume their bodies, and waste their estates, and deny themselves the pleasures of the flesh, as many heathen have done, for the knowledge of nature, of the heavenly bodies and their motions, of the sea and its ebbing and flowing, of the earth and the creatures thereon; when after all their search, they were still at a loss; and for all the knowledge they attained, they proved but learned dunces? What wouldst thou then do for the knowledge of the God of nature, of the mighty possessor of heaven and earth, of him to whom all things are less than nothing, of him the knowledge of whom will make thee wise to salvation? O friend, this is the only knowledge worth seeking, worth getting, worth prizing, worth glorying in: Jer. 9:23, 24, 'Thus saith the Lord, Let not the wise man glory in his wisdom, neither let the mighty man glory in his might, nor the rich man glory in his riches.' Worldly knowledge, strength, wealth, are not worth glorying in; what then is? The next verse tells you: 'But let him that glorieth, glory in this, (in what?) that he understandeth and knoweth me, that I am the Lord,' &c. This is a jewel that a man may boast of, and glory in, that he knoweth me, that I am the Lord.

There is an excellency in all knowledge. Knowledge is the eye of the soul, to direct it in its motions; it is the lamp, the light of the soul, set up by God himself to guide it in its actions. The understanding of man is the candle of the Lord, Prov. 20:27. Without knowledge, the soul is but a dungeon of darkness and blackness, full of confusion and terror; but there is an incomparable excellency in the knowledge of this incomparable God. The object doth elevate and heighten the act. There is a vast difference between the knowledge of earthly things and heavenly things, between the knowledge of wise, strong, faithful, merciful, just, holy men, and the only wise, omnipotent, unchangeable, righteous, most holy God. Only, before I proceed to the urging this use, I would desire thee, reader, to take notice what knowledge of God it is which I am pressing thee to labour for. It is not a mere notional speculative knowledge, though a knowledge of apprehension is a duty, and necessary, Eph. 5:17; Ps. 143:8; Heb. 8:9, 10, but an experimental knowledge: 'Thou hast made me to know wisdom in my secret parts,' Ps. 51:6. The heart is called the secret part, because known only to God, 1 Kings 8:39; such a knowledge as affecteth the heart with love to him, and fear of him, and hatred of what is contrary to him; true knowledge takes the heart as well as takes the head, Ps. 1:6; 1 Kings 8:38; Phil. 3:10; and influenceth the life: 1 John 2:4, 'He that saith, I know him, and keepeth not his commandments, is a liar, and the truth is not in him,' Col. 1:9, 10; John 10:4, 5. Right knowledge, though it begin at the head, doth not end there, but falls down upon the heart to affect that, and floweth out in the life to order and regulate that: Col. 1:10, 'We pray for you, that ye might be filled with the knowledge of his will, in all wisdom and spiritual understanding;' for what end, and to what purpose? 'That ye might walk worthy of the Lord unto all pleasing, being fruitful in every good work.'

To enforce this use, I shall give thee two or three motives, and as many means.

To encourage thee to study the knowledge of this God, consider these three properties of it.

(1). The true knowledge of this God will be a sanctifying knowledge. If thou hast anything of a man, I mean of reason in thee, holiness, which was thy primitive perfection, which is the image of the incomparable God, and will fit thee for his special love and eternal embraces, will be a strong and cogent argument with thee. Now this knowledge of God will conform thee to God, render thee like unto him, who is the pattern and standard of all excellency. As I said before, knowledge is the eye by which we see God, and the vision of God causeth an assimilation to him: 'But we all with open face beholding as in a glass the glory of the Lord, are changed into the same image, from glory to glory, even as by the Spirit of our God,' 2 Cor. 3:18. The blackamore that often looked on beautiful pictures brought forth a beautiful son. We are often changed into the postures and fashions, yea, and dispositions, of those whom we much converse with on earth. Surely, then, acquaintance with the gracious and holy God will make us in some measure to resemble him.

Other knowledge pollutes and defiles the soul. Oftentimes, the more men pick the lock of nature's cabinet, and look into her riches and treasury, her secrets and mysteries, the more atheistical they are, and forgetful of the God of nature. Hence *religio medici*[37] is irreligion. They see so much of the operations of nature, that they ascribe the principal efficiency to the instrument. And hence the wisdom of the philosophers, counted the wisest men in the world, is folly, 1 Cor. 3:19; and though they professed themselves to be wise, yet they became fools, and were guilty of all manner of wickedness, Rom. 1:22, to the end. And what was the reason but this, they knew not God, with all their knowledge? 1 Cor. 1:21.

Ignorant heads are ever accompanied with irreligious hearts, and both are attended with atheistical lives, Eph. 4:18. The apostle tells us of the heathen, that they were estranged from the life of God, a holy life, through the ignorance that was in them, because of the blindness of their hearts. So Hosea 4:1–4. But the knowledge of God purifieth the soul. As the sun conveyeth heat along with its light, so grace is multiplied through the knowledge of God, 2 Pet. 1:2. When Moses had conversed with God in the mount, his face shone, that the Jews could not behold him. When a soul hath once acquainted himself with the blessed God, his life will shine with holiness; therefore David counselleth his son Solomon to know the God of his fathers, and to serve him with a perfect heart and willing mind: first to know him, then to serve him, 1 Chron. 28:9.

This knowledge must needs be a sanctifying knowledge, because it renders sin abominable, the world contemptible, God honourable, and the soul the more humble.

The knowledge of God will render sin most abominable to the soul; it renders sin to be exceeding sinful. The miseries that befall us in our estates, names, bodies, souls, nay, all the curses of the law and torments of the damned, do not discover the ugly, loathsome features, and monstrous deformed nature of sin, like the knowledge of this incomparable God. Job confesseth his sin: chap. 42:2, 'I uttered things that I understood not;' nay, he abhorreth himself for his sin, ver. 5. But whence came he, who sometime justified himself too much, now to abhor himself? He gives us the reason or cause of it: 'I have heard of thee by the hearing of the ear,' I had some knowledge of thee before, 'but now mine eyes see thee,' I now have a clearer and fuller knowledge of thee, 'wherefore I abhor myself, and repent in dust and ashes.' The more we know the greatest good, the more we shall hate the greatest evil.

---

[37] "Religion of the physician," also the title of a 1643 psychological self-portrait by Sir Thomas Browne.

The knowledge of God will render the world contemptible to a Christian. None undervalue the creature but those who have had a sight of the Creator; neither can any trample on the riches, honours, and pleasures of this world, but those who know him who is the riches, and honours, and pleasures of the other world. They who never saw the sun, wonder at a candle; and they who never knew the blessed God, wonder at, and are fond of poor low things, mean, small, pitiful things on earth. But the whole world, with all its crowns, and sceptres, and diadems, and delights, is but a dunghill to him that hath seen the incomparable God. Moses could refuse the honour of being the adopted child of a king's heir, reject the pleasures of Pharaoh's court, and prefer the reproaches of Christ before all the treasures of Egypt, when he had once got a sight of the incomparable God: Heb. 11:25–27, 'For he saw him that was invisible.'

The knowledge of God will render God more honourable in our esteems. The more we know of many things and persons, the more we slight and despise them; the more we know sin, the more we loathe it; the more we know ourselves, the more we abhor ourselves; but the more we know God, the more we love him, and the more we admire him. The reason of all the contempt and affronts which we offer to God is our ignorance of him. The whole world lieth in wickedness, as a beast in its dung, or vermin in their slime, 1 John 5:19; but the reason is what Christ speaks: John 17:25, 'Father, the world hath not known thee;' for the apostle saith, 'had they known, they would never have crucified the Lord of glory,' 1 Cor. 2:8. They who know God, cannot but see infinite reason why they should love, and fear, and honour, and please him all their days. Why, do you think, is God so much wondered at, and worshipped in his church, more than in other parts of the world? Why doth he inhabit their highest praises, Ps. 22:3, and greatest blessings and thanksgivings, but because he is known more there than in other parts of the world? In Judah is God known, therefore his name is great, his name alone is excellent in Israel, Ps. 76:1.

The knowledge of God makes us humble. We never are so low in our own eyes as when we see the most high God. The more we know of men that are more vain, and foolish, and wicked than ourselves, the more we are exalted and puffed up; but the more we know of God, of the great God, the incomparable God, the most holy God, to whom we are as nothing, less than nothing, worse than nothing, the more we abase ourselves.

When David is acquainted with the excellency of God:—'O Lord, my Lord, how excellent is thy name in all the earth, and thy glory is above the heavens!' Ps. 8:1—what low, little, diminutive thoughts hath he of himself and others; ver. 4, 'What is man? Or, what is the son of man?' What a poor, pitiful, contemptible thing is man! What a vain, empty, insignificant nothing is the son of man! We are ashamed of our rush candles, or glowworms, and hide our heads in the presence of the sun. The holiest man abhors himself for his unholiness before the most holy God. So Job 25:2, 'Dominion and fear are with him;' ver. 3, 'There is no number of his armies;' ver. 5, 'Behold even to the moon, and it shineth not, and the stars are not pure in his sight: how much less man that is a worm, and the son of man that is a worm,' ver. 6. A worm is the most despicable, contemptible creature; every beast trampleth on it: such a creature is man in his own apprehensions, when he once understandeth the incomparable God.

When Isaiah had seen the Lord of hosts, though he were a holy man, he crieth out, 'I am undone, I am a man of unclean lips, for mine eyes have seen the Lord of hosts,' Isa. 6:3, 4. He never saw so much of his own uncleanness, as when he saw him in whose presence the heavens are unclean. Other knowledge, like wind in a bladder, puffeth up, 1 Cor. 8:2, but the knowledge of God, as fire nigh the bladder, shrinks and shrivels it up to nothing.

(2). The knowledge of God is a satisfying knowledge. A man may know much of creatures, and the more he knoweth the more unquiet and restless he is; his knowledge, as wind to the stomach, may fill, and pain, and trouble him, but cannot satisfy him; for creatures are not that savoury meat which the heaven-born spiritual immortal soul of man would have, and must have, if ever it be contented. The greatest students, who have wearied and tired out their brains and bodies in the search of nature's secrets, have found by experience, that they 'spent their strength for what is not bread, and their labour for what will not satisfy;' and they have known the truth of the wise man's saying, 'He that increaseth knowledge increaseth sorrow,' Eccles. 1:18.

That knowledge which satisfieth must be of an object that is suitable, in its spirituality, to the nature of the soul; in its all-sufficiency, to the manifold necessities of the soul; and in its immortality, to the duration of the soul; if either of these be wanting in it, the soul cannot receive satisfaction by it, because without all these the soul cannot be perfectly happy; and till it find that which can make it perfectly happy, it will be restless. If it meet with an object that is suitable to its nature, yet if it be not answerable to all its wants, it will still be complaining, wherein it is unsupplied, and so un-quiet. If it meet with an object that is suitable to its nature, and answerable to all its wants, yet if it be not eternal, it must needs be full of fears and troubles in the forethoughts of its amission of so great a good, which would imbitter the present possession of it; for the soul being incorruptible and immortal itself, cannot but desire that good which will run parallel with its own life; and if it desire it nothing will fully satisfy it till it obtain such a good. Now nothing in this world is suitable to the soul's nature—the soul is spiritual, the things of this world are carnal—nor answerable to the various indigencies of the soul—the soul's wants are many, and in a manner infinite; besides they are spiritual, as pardon of sin, peace with God, peace of conscience, &c., when the good things of this life are particular, finite, and bodily—nor equal to the soul's duration—the soul will abide and continue after millions of ages and generations, forever and ever; but this world passeth away, and all the good things thereof. But this God, whom I am persuading thee, reader, to know and acquaint thyself with, is in all these respects perfect, and so will satisfy thy soul. God is a spiritual good—a spirit, John 4:23, the Father of spirits, and so suitable to the nature of thy soul. He is a universal good, all good, and so answerable to the many wants of thy soul. He is an eternal good, a good that never dieth, never fadeth—a good that only hath immortality, and so is equal to thy soul's duration; therefore the disciple crieth out to Christ, 'Shew us the Father, and it sufficeth,' John 14:8; and David tells us, that he is fully pleased in having God for his portion, Ps. 14:5, 6.

Give any man both that which he would have, and that which he should have, and he is contented. If indeed you give a man what he would have, supposing it be that which he should not have, his desires being depraved and vitiated, he cannot be contented when he hath what he desired, because lusts are unsatiable, and sinful desires never satisfied; thence the heathen emperors had their inventors of new pleasures, and possibly that may be the meaning of that place, Rom. 1:28. The heathen, wearied with common, invented unnatural delights. But give a man what he would have, suppose it be what he should have, his desires being rectified, and he is then at ease and rest.

He who knoweth God aright is fully satisfied in him; when he once drinketh of the 'fountain of living waters,' he thirsteth no more after other objects, Job 4:14. Though the soul still desireth to know more of God, till it come to that place where it shall know as it is known, as David, though satisfied with his portion, Ps. 16:4, 5, yet thirsted after more of it, Ps. 63:1, 2, yet it is quiet and contented in God. And indeed the sweetness which it tasteth in acquaintance with the incomparable God, makes it long after nearer and fuller acquaintance with him. When Moses was once acquainted with God, he begs that he might see and know more of his glory; and the reason is, because while God is the object, there can be no satiety, he being the God of all joy and consolation; neither can there be such a full acquaintance as to cease desires after further acquaintance, he being an object still too great for the faculties to comprehend. The desires of the glorified are without anxiety, because they are satisfied in the object of their desires; and their satisfaction or enjoyment is without satiety or loathing, because they see still infinite cause to desire him.

When the soul once comes to know God, as the needle touched with the loadstone, when it turns to the north, it is then quiet, though before, like the dove, it hovered up and down over the waters of this world, and could find no rest. This knowledge, if right, diffuseth into the soul a sweet tranquillity, silent peace, secret settled calmness, besides a ravishing prevision, and blessed fore-fruition of its fuller acquaintance in the other life.

(3). The knowledge of God is a saving knowledge. Many perish for all their great knowledge of creatures; their knowledge may light them to the more dismal chambers of death, of blackness of darkness forever, Job 15:24. And indeed their knowledge, like many pigs of silver in a vessel sinking, presseth them the deeper into hell; but the knowledge of God is saving; God will know him in the other world, who knows him in this. He will be so far from knowing them hereafter who are ignorant of him here, that he will come 'in flaming fire to render vengeance on them that know not God,' 2 Thes. 1:7, 8. But he will own them, and take acquaintance with them then, that own him and are acquainted with him now: Ps. 91:14, 'I will set him on high, because he hath known my name.' God will set him as high as heaven, who knoweth his name on earth. Reader, it is as much worth as heaven to thee to know this incomparable God. 'This is life eternal, to know thee the only true God, and Jesus Christ whom thou hast sent,' John 17:3. It is the morning, though not the meridian of heaven; it is the bud, though not the ripe fruit of glory; it is the seed, though not the harvest of the inheritance above, to know the true God and Jesus Christ. This knowledge is of the same nature, though not of the same measure, with that in the other world, Eph. 4:13. Now the Christian knoweth as a child, then he shall know as a man; now he seeth God as it were at a distance through the prospective glass of faith, but then he shall see God face to face. 'Now we see through a glass darkly, but then face to face; now we know in part, but then we shall know as we are known,' 1 Cor. 13:12.

XXIII

THE MEANS OF ACQUAINTANCE WITH GOD; A SENSE OF OUR IGNORANCE; ATTENDANCE ON THE WORD; FERVENT PRAYER

The means which I shall offer as helpful to the attainment of this knowledge of God, are these:

i. Be sensible of thine ignorance of him. A conceited scholar is no good learner. He that thinks he knoweth enough already, will never be beholden to a master to teach him more: 'Seest thou a man wise in his own conceit? There is more hope of a fool than of him,' Prov. 26:12. This is that which locked up the Pharisees in the dark dungeon of ignorance: they are blind; truth itself called them blind, Mat. 22:16, 17. But they conceited their eyes were good, and so neglected the means of curing them. 'Ye say ye see;' I do not say ye see, but ye conceit so, 'therefore your sin remaineth,' John 9:40, 41, therefore your ignorance continueth. When ignorance and confidence, which are often twins, go together, the condition of a man is helpless; partly because such a person will not take that pains in reading, and praying, and conference, and meditation, without which the knowledge of God cannot be had; Dan. 12:4, 'Many shall run to and fro, and knowledge shall be increased.' It is an allusion to merchants, that run to this and that port, to sell out and take in commodities; or to a tradesman, that runs to this and that mart or place to buy and sell, whereby their stocks are increased. But a conceited man will never labour thus for that which he thinks he hath already. 'If thou diggest as for silver, and searchest as for hid treasure, then thou shalt understand the fear of the Lord, and attain the knowledge of God,' Prov. 2:4, 5. Men count digging hard work, and will sweat at it when they dig for silver: such diligence must they use who will get the knowledge of God. But though poor men, who are sensible of their want of the knowledge of God, and of their woeful condition thereby, will work to preserve themselves from perishing; yet rich men, who think they can do well enough without it, will spare their pains, partly, because all knowledge must be obtained from God by fervent prayer; and a conceited man will neither be instant with God for it, nor will God give it to him. God is the God of knowledge, 1 Sam. 2:2; and from him all true saving knowledge cometh; Prov. 2:6, 'The Lord giveth wisdom, out of his mouth cometh knowledge and understanding.' As none can see the sun by candle-light, but by its own light, so none can know God savingly by the light of nature, but by light derived from himself. Now a conceited person will not go to God for knowledge. What need I? Thinks he; I have enough already. Poverty is a friend to prayer: 'The poor useth entreaties,' Prov. 18:23; but pride or conceitedness is an enemy to prayer; 'The wicked, through the pride of his countenance, will not seek after God,' Ps. 10:4. Who will beg that of his neighbour which he is confident he hath at home? Neither will God undertake the instruction of proud scholars: 'The humble he will teach, the meek he will guide in judgment,' Ps. 25:9. Such as are willing to be taught will be thankful for their learning, and are fitted for guidance and direction; but conceited persons are quite contrary. Therefore, reader, beware of this mist in which many miscarry. 'He that thinketh he knoweth anything, knoweth nothing as he ought to know,' 1 Cor. 8:2; but labour to get thine hearted affected with thine ignorance, and the woeful consequents of it, Ps. 95:10, 11. This will be a good step to knowledge. The apostle gives the same direction: 1 Cor. 3:18, 'If any man seem to be wise, let him become a fool that he may be wise.' If thou seemest to be knowing, be ignorant in thy own sense and feeling and apprehension, that thou mayest be knowing. Our Lord Jesus gives the same counsel to the sick and dying Laodiceans, Rev. 3:17, 18, and acquaints her that her ignorance of her ignorance, and conceitedness of her knowledge, was the great hindrance of her recovery.

ii. Study much the works, and especially the word of God. The works of God are a book wherein you may read of him, and by which you may hear of him. 'The heavens declare his glory,' Ps. 19:1; 'The earth is full of his goodness,' Ps. 33:5. As the shadow hath some proportion to the body to which it relates, so the works of God are some representation of the wise, powerful, gracious God to whom they belong. Rom. 1:19, 21, 'The invisible things of God are seen by the things that are made, even his eternal power and godhead;' therefore consider the works of the Lord, and the operations of his hands.

The word of God is a glass, wherein thou mayest see his beauty and grace and glory, and so see him as to be transformed into his likeness, 2 Cor. 3:18. In the works of God you may see his steps, the prints of his feet; they are therefore called his paths and his goings, Ps. 77:19. But in his word we may see his face, the comeliness of his countenance, how lovely and amiable he is; therefore it is called a glass, 2 Cor. 3:18: so that, as the sight of a man's face helpeth and conduceth more to our knowledge of him than the sight of his steps, so the word of God is a far greater means of our acquaintance with him than the works of creation and providence. Therefore, I say, study especially the word of God. The Scripture is the key of knowledge, Luke 11:52, and unlocks the mysteries which were kept hid from ages and generations, and opens the secrets of heaven to thy soul. It is therefore called light, Ps. 119:105, and a lamp, Prov. 6:23, because it discovers hidden things, helps thee to see what thou canst not without it, and directs thee in thy motions and actions. David had more knowledge than his enemies, and they were subtle; than his teachers, and they were no dwarfs in knowledge—such as Gad and Nathan; than the ancient, and with 'the ancient is wisdom, and in length of days is understanding,' Job 12:12, 13; and what was the means of it? 'For thy testimonies are my meditation,' Ps. 119:97–99. The gospel is the eyesalve by which the blind come to see, Ps. 19:7. The fragrancy and attractiveness of the incomparable God increaseth up and down in the world as the gospel is propagated. 'Thanks be to God, who maketh manifest the savour of his knowledge (the knowledge of God, like a rich perfume, causeth and leaveth a fragrant odoriferous scent wherever it comes) by us (the ministers of the gospel as the instruments hereof) in every place,' 2 Cor. 2:14. The ministry of the word is the chariot of the Sun of righteousness, whereby he conveyeth the light of the knowledge of God to the world. Therefore attend on preaching, and give diligence to reading: 'Search the Scriptures, for they are they that testify of me,' John 5:39.

iii. Be frequent and fervent with God to give thee the knowledge of himself. There is a twofold light requisite to bodily vision: a light in the eye, (a blind man cannot see at noon-day;) and a light in the air, (the best eye cannot see in the dark:) so there is a twofold light requisite to the effectual sight of God—viz., the light of the word and the light of the Spirit; the word cannot do it without the Spirit, and the Spirit will not do it without the word; where the word is afforded both are needful. 'There is a spirit in man,' a passive receptiveness as a capable subject, 'but the inspiration of the Almighty giveth understanding,' Job 32:8.

All natural abilities, all acquired endowments, all the reading and learn-ing, all the teachers and tutors in the world, cannot help one poor soul to the saving knowledge of God. It is God that teacheth man knowledge, Ps. 94:10. He who made light in the first creation, only can cause light in the new creation; 2 Cor. 4:6, 'But God, who caused light to shine out of darkness, hath shined in our hearts, to give the light of the knowledge of the glory of God, in the face of Jesus Christ.' He that at first said, 'Let there be light,' when darkness covered the face of the world, 'and there was light,' a cor-poreal light, can command spiritual light, and the knowledge of his glory in the face of Christ, who is the express image of his person. Therefore the apostle betakes himself to God for the gift, 'Praying that the God of our Lord Jesus Christ would give unto you the spirit of wisdom and revelation, in the knowledge of him,' &c., Eph. 1:17, 18; so David often, Ps. 119:18, 34, 35, 125, 143, 144; Rev. 3:18. Reader, art thou blind? Take the counsel of thy Saviour. Go to him for eyesalve that thou mayest see, and be confident he that bids thee come to him for that will bid thee welcome when thou comest, Rev. 3:18. 'None knoweth the Father but the Son, and he to whom the Son will reveal him,' Mat. 11:27.

Therefore whoever thou art that sittest in darkness, and in the shadow of death, go to the sun for light, go to the Sun of righteousness, in whom are all the treasures of wisdom and knowledge, Col. 2:9, for the light of the knowledge of God. Dost thou not know the sinfulness and misery of a blind dark state, that vengeance is the fruit of this ignorance? Ps. 79:6. That God will pour out his wrath upon them that know him not? Go, therefore, as the blind man, to the Lord Jesus Christ. Cry, sigh, mourn, pray: 'Jesus, thou son of David, have mercy on me;' though he hear not presently, hold on, con-tinue instant in prayer; though the devil and flesh rebuke thee, as the mul-titude him, yet hold on, call louder, 'Jesus, thou son of David, have mercy on me,' Mark 10:47; 'Lord, that I might receive my sight,' ver. 51; and doubt not but he will have pity on thee, as he had on him, and touch thine eye, and give thee to see the things of thy peace; for thine encouragement thou hast his promise: Jer. 24:7, 'I will give them an heart to know me, that I am the Lord;' Jer. 31:34, 'They shall all know me, from the least to the greatest.' So James 1:6; Hosea 2:20; Heb. 8:8, 9. Oh, with what hope mayest thou sue these bonds and plead these promises, when he that made them is a God that cannot lie, Titus 1:2, and therefore cannot but perform them! Again, observe how kindly he took it of Solomon, when he bid Solomon ask what he would, that he asked wisdom, 2 Chron. 1:10. Give me wisdom and knowledge, saith Solomon: and the thing which Solomon asked pleased the Lord, 1 Kings 3:10. And the Lord said unto Solomon, 'Because this was in thine heart, because thou hast not asked riches, nor honour, nor the life of thine enemies, nor long life, wisdom and knowledge is granted to thee, and I will give thee wealth and honour,' ver. 11. When a poor creature, sensible of its blindness and darkness, lieth at the feet of God, begging spiritual light and sight, the heart of the Redeemer is taken with such a request, and subscribes the petition with, Wisdom and knowledge is granted to thee. Be but diligent, reader, in the use of these means, and thou mayest be confident of success: 'If thou criest after knowledge, and liftest up thy voice for understanding; if thou seekest her as silver, and searchest for her as for hidden treasure, then shalt thou understand the fear of the Lord, and find the knowledge of God; for the Lord giveth wisdom, out of his mouth cometh knowledge and understanding,' Prov. 2:3-6.

XXIV

EXHORTATION TO CHOOSE THIS INCOMPARABLE GOD FOR OUR PORTION; WITH SOME MOTIVES THEREUNTO

2. If this God be such an incomparable God, then choose this God for thy portion, and take him for thy happiness. Is it possible for thee to read so much of the incomparableness of God in his being, attributes, works, and word, and not desire him? Thou canst hardly see an excellent person, but thou art wishing him for thy friend, thy companion; nor an excellent estate, but thou art wishing it were thine inheritance, thy portion; and canst thou hear of him who is excellency itself originally, Job 13:11, the spring and standard of all excellency in others, whose name alone is excellent, Ps. 148:13, and not wish, Oh that this incomparable God were my friend, my father, my head, my husband, my lot, my portion? Who will give me to drink of the water of the well of Bethlehem? Oh, who will help me to drink of the well of salvation, of the fountain of living waters, of the pure river that floweth from the throne of God and the Lamb? Canst thou hear so much of his worth, though infinitely short, and not desire him? Is it possible for a rational creature to read of such a bottomless treasure, of such boundless pleasure, of such an infinite inconceivable good, and not covet the enjoyment of it? O man, where are thy wits? Whither art thou fallen? Art thou a man or a beast? Ah, didst thou know the gift of God, and what it is that is offered thee, thou wouldst scorn the highest honours, sweetest carnal delights, greatest riches, yea, trample upon all the crowns and kingdoms of this world for it. It is an ineffable privilege that thou art a creature capable of so vast a happiness, it is a special favour that thou hast leave to aspire after such an immense inheritance; and when it is tendered to thee, wilt thou refuse it? Wilt thou neglect it? Oh, wilt thou not give it all acceptation?

Having spoken in another treatise to this particular, I shall here only offer two or three things to thy serious thoughts, and proceed to a third exhortation.

(1). Consider, what is offered thee, when the incomparable God is offered thee for thy portion. And truly, to explain this head fully, would require the pen, yea, exceed the skill, of an angel. None can tell what God is, but God himself. All the sheets in the explication of the doctrine speak somewhat of him, but not the thousand thousandth part of that excellency that is in him. Reader, I may tell thee, when God is offered thee, the greatest good that ever was, that ever will be, that ever can be, is offered thee; there never was, or can be, the like offered thee; more than heaven and earth, than both worlds, than millions of worlds, is offered thee. This God who is offered thee is the King of kings, the Lord of lords, the God of gods, the blessed and glorious potentate, the first cause, the original being, self-sufficient, all-sufficient, absolutely perfect, incapable of any addition or diminution. This God who is offered thee is the high and lofty, One that inhabiteth eternity every moment, to whom a thousand years, yea, millions of ages, are but as one day, as one moment, whose duration is incapable of the least accession, who is boundless in his being, omnipotent in his power, unsearchable in his wisdom, inconceivable in his grace, and infinite in all his perfections. He dwelleth in that light that is inaccessible; before him angels, the highest of creatures, vail their faces; to him the whole creation is less than nothing, and vanity. This God who is offered thee made all things of nothing, supports all things, influenceth all things, and is all things, and infinitely more than all things. He is so needful a good that thou art undone without him. This was the misery of the heathen on earth, Eph. 2:12, and of the damned in hell, Mat. 25:41, the very hell of hell. He is so plentiful a good that thou art perfectly happy in him, Ps. 144:15, thou needest no more. He is the heaven of heavens, Ps. 16:11, the safest refuge. O friend, what dost thou think of having this God for thy portion? Is it not worth the while to have this God for thy God? Wilt thou not say, 'Forasmuch as there is none like unto thee, O Lord; thou art great, and thy name is great: who would not fear thee, O king of nations'? Jer. 10:6, 7. Again, the God who is offered thee is the well of salvation, the Lord of life, the God of all consolation, a hive of sweetness, a paradise of pleasure, a heaven of joy. He is the richest grace, the dearest love, the surest friend, the highest honour, the vastest treasure, the exactest beauty, the chiefest good, and the fullest felicity. He is one that can enlarge and suit all thy faculties, relieve and answer all thy necessities, fill up and satisfy all the capacities of thy heaven-born soul. God is a good which Christ died to purchase for thee, Eph. 2:13; 1 Pet. 3:18. And surely if Christ thought him worth his blood, he is worthy thine acceptance. God is a comprehensive universal good, not one, but all good; riches, honours, pleasures, friends, relations, health, life, earth, heaven, this world, the other world, all the good of both worlds, and infinitely more; and art thou not covetous of such wealth, that is better worth than both worlds? Phil. 4:19; Ps. 23:1; Gen. 17:1. God is an everlasting good, a good that will stand by thee, and abide with thee when all other good things shall fail thee, 1 Tim. 6:7; Ps. 73:25. He is that good which thou wouldst have if thou art well in thy wits: he is that good which thou shouldst have if thou answerest the end of thy creation; he is that good which thou must have, if thou art not eternally miserable; he is the only suitable satisfying good, which hits the nature, and fits the desire of the rational creature. O reader, I say again, what dost thou think of having this incomparable God for thy God? Surely by this time thy heart may well melt into astonishment that he will allow thee to seek so matchless a portion. Well, what sayest thou to him? Is it not worth the while to have him for thine, to whom thou wilt call in the day of distress, to whom thou wilt cry in a dying hour, when thy soul stands quivering on thy lips, ready to take its flight into the unknown regions of the other world, when devils will be waiting to seize it, as soon as ever it leaves the body, to hale it to the unquenchable flames of hell, when thy friends and relations shall be weeping and wailing by thee, but unable to afford thy dying body the least cordial, or thy departing soul the least comfort? Ah, friend, what wilt thou do in such an hour, which is hastening on thee, without the incomparable God? Believe it, though thou mayest live without him, thou canst not die, without an infinite horror, without him. Is it not worth the while to have him for thine, to whom thou must stand or fall forever, from whose mouth thy sentence of eternal absolution or condemnation must come, and who shall judge thee to thine unchangeable state of life or death? Though thou mayest think thou canst do well enough at this day with the world for thy portion; yet what wilt thou do at that day, when the world shall be in a flame, if God be not thy portion? Art thou willing or not, to have this God for thine? What sayest thou? Canst thou find in thine heart to deprive thy precious soul of such an inestimable treasure, and to leave it naked in the other world to the cruelty of devils, and the dreadful curses of the law? Methinks, though I have spoken little, yet I have said enough, to one that will but let his reason judge, to draw out thy most earnest desires after this incomparable God.

(2). Consider upon what terms thou mayest have this God for thy God. You may possibly think that so boundless a good must cost you very dear, and the price must be vast of a pearl that is so matchless; but lo, to thy comfort, all the condition which God requireth of thee is only to accept him heartily and thankfully in his Son. Canst thou have anything cheaper? Wouldst thou desire him in his terms to fall lower? Nay, is it possible so to do, and make thee happy? Nor can he be thine unless thou receivest him for thine. It is a poor favour that is not worth acceptance. Do but take him for your happiness, and you shall have him for your happiness.

Thou givest more for thy bread, thy clothes, thy house, for the needful comforts that are for the support of thy frail body, than thou needest give for the great, glorious, incomprehensible, incomparable God. Thou payest money for them, but thou mayest have him without money and without price. One would think that the equity of the condition should both amaze thee and allure thee. Consider, I say, God doth not require of thee things impossible to thee; he doth not say, If thou wilt remove mountains, dry up oceans, stop the course of nature, create worlds, I will then be thine, as great as I am; he doth not say, If thou wilt satisfy my justice, answer the demands of my law, merit my love and favour, then I will be thy God. No; he himself hath done all this for thee by the death of his Son; all he desireth is, that thou wouldst accept him in his Son for thy God. Nay, he doth not require of thee anything that is barbarous or cruel, as the heathen deities did, by the devil, of their worshippers. He doth not say, If you will lance and mangle your bodies, as Baal's priests did; if ye will go barefoot in sackcloth long and tedious pilgrimages, as the papists do; if ye will offer your children in the fire, and give the fruit of your bodies for the sins of your souls, as some did, then I will be your God. Again, he doth not require of thee things that are chargeable, to offer the best and chief of thy flock daily in sacrifice to him; nor, as he once did of the young man, to sell all that thou hast, and give it to the poor; nor, as idolaters, to lay down such a part of thy estate for thy pardon; but he only requires that thou wouldst take the Lord for thy God; and wilt thou not do it? Canst thou deny him and thy poor soul so reasonable, so equitable a request?

As the servant said to Naman, 'If the prophet had commanded thee some great thing, wouldst not thou have done it? How much more then when he only saith, Wash, and be clean?' So say I to thee; if God had commanded the greatest things imaginable, wouldst thou not to thy power have done them, that thou mightest enjoy the blessed God for thy eternal portion? How much more then when he only saith, 'Thou shalt have no other God before me'? O reader, do but observe that first command, which contains the sum both of thy duty and felicity, and thou art made, thou art a blessed man forever. Take the true God in Jesus Christ for thy God, prize him as thy God, love him as thy God, honour him as thy God, and obey him as thy God, and he will be thy God forever. Do but as much for the true God as the covetous man doth for his wealth, which is his god, as the intemperate man for his belly, which is his god; they give their highest esteem, their choicest affections, and their greatest service to that which they take for their god. And surely the true God is more worthy hereof, and will requite thee best for them.

(3). Consider for what end God offereth himself to thee. I would not have thee mistake, because God out of his infinite pity to his miserable creatures, is instant and urgent with them to accept of him, to think therefore that God hath any need of thee, or seeketh his own happiness therein; I tell thee, if thou hadst no more need of God than he hath of thee, thou mayest let him alone. No; it is purely for thy good, for thy real and eternal good, that he offereth himself to thee; he needeth thy service no more than he doth the service of the damned, of the devils; and he knoweth how to make use of thee for his own glory, as he doth of them, if thou foolishly rejectest his offer of himself. Thy righteousness will not help him, Job 22:2, 3, nor thy wickedness hurt him, Job 35:2. He offereth himself to thee, not that he may be blessed by thee, but that he may be bountiful to thee. It is thy good, not his own, that he looks at; the felicity of accepting him is thine own, and the misery of neglecting him is thine own, Prov. 9:12. Men call customers to them, press them with many arguments and entreaties to buy, that they may enrich themselves by their customers; but God calls men to buy of him, not to enrich himself— he is as rich, and perfect and happy as he can be—but to enrich themselves; I counsel thee, saith Christ to his lukewarm church, to buy of me gold. Why? That he may get somewhat by her, and enrich himself? No; that thou mayest be rich; that thou, not I, mayest be rich. Now, reader, ponder it seriously, it is wholly for thy own good, that thou mayest escape wrath and death, and attain heaven and life, that God is pleased once more to offer himself to thee. What is thy mind about his offer? Wilt thou have him for thy portion or no? Is there anything unreasonable in his desire or demands? Doth not thy eternal felicity depend on thine acceptance of him? What sayest thou? Wilt thou have God for thy portion, or wilt thou have the devil for thy portion? Thou shalt have an eternal portion, good or bad. The worldling's portion of good things is but for this world, and the godly man's portion of evil things is but for this world; both have immortal souls, which will abide in the other world forever; and their souls must have immortal portions to abide with them there forever. Therefore, reader, consider what thou doest, either thou must take God, in and through Christ, for thy portion forever, or hell and death and wrath and devils for thy portion forever; one of the two is the portion of all the sons and daughters of Adam. If thou wilt still prefer the world before God, and love the creature above God, and please thy flesh more than God; when once thou appearest in the other world, God will rain on thee 'fire and brimstone, and a horrible tempest: this will be the portion of thy cup,' Ps. 11:6. But if now thou acceptest him in his Son (for there is no making God thy friend but by Christ) for thy chiefest good and happiness, when all thy friends shall leave thee, and dearest relations forsake thee, yea, when 'thy flesh and thy heart shall fail thee, God will be the strength of thine heart, and thy portion forever.' O friend, consider what I have said in this use, and the Lord give thee understanding, that thou mayest know when thou art well offered, and be wise on this side the other world.

XXV

EXHORTATION TO GIVE GOD THE GLORY OF HIS INCOMPARABLE EXCELLENCY; WITH SOME CONSIDERATIONS TO ENFORCE IT

If God be such an incomparable God, give him the glory and honour of his incomparable excellencies; his incomparable perfections must have incomparable praises. 'Praise him,' saith the psalmist, 'according to his excellent greatness,' Ps. 150:2. But, alas! What tongue, what understanding of men or angels can do it, can praise him according to his excellent greatness? But though we cannot praise him according to the utmost of his excellencies, we must praise him according to the utmost of our abilities. The highest God, Ps. 92:1, must have the highest praises: Ps. 149:6, 'The high praises of God are in their mouths.' The greatest God, Ps. 145:3, must have our greatest praises; 'Great is the Lord, and greatly to be praised.' Low or little praises are a dispraise to one so eminently, so infinitely, high and great.

Ordinary commendations of an extraordinary person are a discommendation to him. 'According to thy name, so, O Lord, is thy praise to the end of the earth,' Ps. 48:10. Therefore his name alone being excellent, Ps. 148:13, his praise alone must be excellent. David tells God, 'I will praise thee yet more and more,' Ps. 71:14. He had already praised him much, but he would endeavour to praise him more; and when he had done so, he would praise him more, and still more. We read of songs of degrees, Ps. 120. and 121. We should ascend in our praises of God by a holy climax, till we come to the highest degree that is possible, and screw up our faculties herein to the utmost pitch that they are capable of.

Praise him for the incomparableness of his being. That he is an independent, all-sufficient, absolutely perfect, incomprehensible, omnipresent, eternal, infinite being, should much affect our hearts. 'Praise ye the Lord, praise him, O ye servants of the Lord, praise the name of the Lord. Blessed be the name of the Lord from this time forth and forever. From the rising of the sun to the going down of the same, the Lord's name is to be praised.' Why? 'The Lord is high above all nations, and his glory above the heavens; who is like to the Lord our God, who dwelleth on high?' Ps. 113:1–5.

Praise him for his incomparableness in his attributes, for the incomparableness of his power: 'O Lord God of hosts, who is a strong Lord like unto thee?' Ps. 89:8. For the incomparableness of his holiness: 'Who is a God like unto thee, glorious in holiness?' Exod. 15:11. For the incomparableness of his mercy: 'Who is a God like unto thee, pardoning iniquity, and passing by the transgressions of the remnant of his heritage, because he delighteth in mercy?'

Praise him for the incomparableness of his words: 'Oh that men would praise the Lord for his goodness, and for his wonderful works to the children of men,' Ps. 107:8, 15, 21, 31, 72:18, and 136:4. Praise him for the work of creation, Ps. 114:1–5; Job 38:4–6. Praise him for his works of providence: Ps. 97:8, 9, 136 throughout, and 107. Praise him especially for the work of redemption: 'Blessed be the Lord God of Israel, who hath visited and redeemed his people,' Luke 1:68; Ps. 9:1; Rev. 15:3.

Praise him for the incomparableness of his word: 'Wonderful are thy testimonies,' Ps. 119:129. How often doth the sweet singer of Israel praise God for them, as a singular kindness! Ps. 147, two last verses. 'He gave his statutes to Moses, his laws and commandments to Jacob. He hath not dealt so with every nation; praise ye the Lord.'

Praise him by admiring him. Wonder at his being, as they of Christ: 'What manner of man is this, that the winds and seas obey him?' Mat. 8:27. What manner of God is this, who knoweth no bounds, no beginning, no succession, no addition? An amazing admiration of him is a high commendation of him. And, indeed, our silent wondering at his perfections is almost all the worship we can give him: Ps. 65:1, 'Praise waiteth for thee, O God, in Sion,'—Heb., 'Praise is silent for thee, O God, in Sion;' not that praise was dumb or tongue-tied in Sion, for praise in no part of the world speaks higher or louder than in Sion; but to shew that when the people of God set themselves to praise him, they are struck with amazement and wonder at his matchless being and beauty, at his infinite excellencies and perfections; and wanting words to express them, they sit down in a silent admiration of them. Thou wouldst wonder at Adam, if he were now alive, for his age. Oh, wonder at him that is from everlasting to everlasting, that is the cause and original of all things, that is what he is, that is, and nothing else is; that is all he is in one indivisible point of eternity.

Wonder at his attributes, admire his holiness. 'Behold, he putteth no trust in his servants, he chargeth the angels with folly,' Job 4:18. Behold, wonder at it. Again, 'Behold, he putteth no trust in his saints; the heavens are not clean in his sight,' Job 15:15. Admire his wisdom; cry out with the apostle, 'Oh the depth of the wisdom and knowledge of God,' Rom. 11:33. Admire his love; 'Behold what manner of love hath the Father loved us with,' 1 John 3:1. Admire his power, that he can do what he will do: 'Who is a strong Lord like unto thee?' Ps. 89:8.

Wonder at his works. Thou art ready to wonder at the rare works of some curious artist; alas! All their works are toys to the works of the mighty Creator and possessor of heaven and earth. 'O Lord, how marvellous are thy works!' Ps. 106:24. His work is honourable and glorious, Ps. 109:3, and worthy thy greatest wonder.

What a piece is the creation! How marvellous! How mysterious! Ps. 8:1–5. 'The heavens declare his glory,' Ps. 19:1, and the earth is 'full of his goodness,' Ps. 104:24. What a work is providence! Read Ps. 104 and 107. How many rarities, curiosities, mysteries, are wrapped up in it, which are only seen in the other world! Ps. 77:19.

What man is this, say they, for he commandeth with authority, and the unclean spirits come out of men? Mark 1:27. What a masterpiece, what rare workmanship indeed is redemption! A work that the angels are always prying into and wondering at, Eph. 3:8; 1 Pet. 1:10.

Wonder at his word. When thou hearest it, dost thou not perceive a majesty and authority aweing thy conscience accompanying it? 'And they were all amazed and astonished at his doctrine,' Luke 4:32. The very officers who were sent to apprehend Christ could not but wonder at his words, and returned to them who set them awork. 'Never man spake as he spake,' John 7:47. There are great things in the law of God, Hosea 8:12; things that are wonderful, Ps. 119:18, which may well be wondered at. And all, saith the evangelist, bare him witness, and 'wondered at the gracious words which proceeded out of his mouth,' Luke 4:22.

Praise him by speaking always highly and honourably of him. If his name alone be excellent, take heed that thou dost not take his excellent name in vain. Thy apprehensions of him must be ever high, and thy expressions of him honourable. Thy tongue is therefore called thy glory, because therewith thou mayest glorify thy God, Ps. 57:8.

Never speak of God rashly or at random, without a serious consideration of whom thou speakest; and let thy expressions of him and to him be becoming his vast perfections; 'Ascribe greatness to our God,' Deut. 32:3.

Speak honourably of his being: so Moses, Exod. 14:11, 'Who is a God like unto thee, glorious in holiness, fearful in praises?' So Solomon, 1 Kings 8:23, 'Lord God of Israel, there is no god like unto thee in heaven above, or in the earth beneath.' So David, 1 Chron. 29:11.

Speak honourably of his attributes, Ps. 68:34; of his power, mercy, truth, justice, wisdom, and holiness; 'Holy, holy, holy, Lord God of hosts,' Isa. 6:3.

Speak honourably of his works: Ps. 86:8, 'Among all the gods there is none like unto thee; neither are there any works like unto thy works,' Ps. 145:10.

Speak honourably of his word. 'The commandments of the Lord are pure,' Ps. 19:7. 'Thy word is very pure. The statutes of the Lord are right,' Ps. 19:10. 'The law is holy, just, and good,' Rom. 7:12. Though Paul's corruption took occasion, by the law's prohibitions, to become the most unruly, as the water at a bridge roars the more for the stop, yet he dares not lay the least fault upon the law, but layeth all upon himself; 'was the law sin? God forbid,' ver. 7. Far be it from me to have the least such thought. No; the law is holy, but I am carnal, sold under sin, ver. 14. So when he speaketh of the gospel, how honourably doth he speak of it! sometimes he calls it the glorious gospel, 2 Cor. 4:4; the mysteries of the gospel, Eph. 6:19; the word of truth, Col. 1:5.

Praise him by walking circumspectly and closely with him. Live always as one that believeth he hath at all times to do with this incomparable God, and is created, and preserved, and redeemed, to shew forth the praise of this God. When the psalmist had admired the incomparableness of this God in his being and doings, Ps. 86:8, he presently subjoins, ver. 9, 'All nations whom thou hast made shall come and glorify thy name, and worship before thee. For thou art great, and dost wondrous things; thou art God alone.' O friend, this incomparable God must have incomparable obedience; 'Be still, and know that I am God,' Ps. 46:10. 'Be still, be quiet; O sinner, cease, forbear any further to offend me, and know that I am God, incomparable in knowledge, acquainted with all thy ways and works, inward, outward, secret, private, public; incomparable in holiness, and perfectly hate all thy wickedness; incomparable in power, able to revenge myself on thee every moment, to turn thee body and soul into hell; incomparable in justice, and will by no means clear the guilty; yet incomparable in mercy, and will accept and receive prodigals, that, sensible of their folly and filthiness, return home to me, their Father, in the Son of my love. Be still, sinner; know this, that I am God; and obey my laws. But I have spoken more fully of this in the informations; only remember that the praise of thy life is the life of thy praise; because hereby thou dost in some measure represent the excellencies of this incomparable God, visible to the world, 1 Pet. 2:9; Mat. 5:18. Offering praise, and ordering the conversation aright, are joined together by God himself, and let not us part them asunder, Ps. 50:23.

To help thee a little, that thou mayest give God the praise of incomparable perfections. Consider—

i. This God is excellency itself; he is not only excellent, Ps. 8:1, and alone excellent, Ps. 148:13, but excellency, Job 13:11, 'should not his excellency make thee afraid?' Nay, he is greatness of excellency, Exod. 15:7, nothing but excellency, 1 John 1:6. Now, think with thyself what honour is due to one that is excellent, alone excellent, excellency itself, and nothing but excellency. Can thy highest honour be high enough, or thy most excellent praises be excellent enough for such an excellency?

ii. This God is the standard of all excellency. Nothing is excellent but because of its relation or likeness to him. Everything is more or less excellent as it is more or less related or conformable to him. Saints are the excellent of the earth, Ps. 16:3; more excellent than their neighbours, Prov. 12:26; but it is because of his affection to them: 'Since thou art precious in my sight thou art honourable,' Isa. 43:4; and because of their relation and likeness to him, Deut. 33:29; 1 Pet. 2:9; Ps. 48:2, 3. The Scriptures are the most excellent of books; none like them. 'I have written unto thee excellent things,' Prov. 22:20. But what is the reason? Surely because they are the word of God, Eph. 3:16; his mind, 2 Cor. 2:17. 'All scripture is given by inspiration of God,' 2 Tim. 3:16. The Sabbath is the most excellent of days, the queen of days, the golden spot of the week, because it is his day, set apart by him, and devoted to him. 'My holy day, the holy of the Lord, honourable,' Isa. 58:13. Grace is excellent, the beauty and glory of the creature, Prov. 4:7; 2 Cor. 3:18; more excellent than gold or fine gold, than rubies or pearls, Prov. 3:14, 15; but why? Because it is his image, it is a conformity to his nature, 2 Pet. 1:4; 2 Cor. 3:18. When the Holy Ghost would render anything excellent, he mentions it with relation to God. The cedars of God, the city of God, the trees of God, the mountains of God, &c.; that is, the most excellent cedars, cities, trees, and mountains.

iii. He is so excellent that even angels veil their faces in his presence. The excellent cherubims and seraphims, who are spotless in their natures, and faultless in their lives, who are the highest and honourablest, and ancientest house of the creation, who, as his special friends and favourites, are allowed to wait on him continually, to behold him face to face, and to enjoy him fully and perfectly, yet these angels veil their faces before him, as it were, ashamed of their starlight in the presence of the sun, and their drops in the presence of the ocean: Isa. 6:1–3, 'I saw the Lord sitting on a throne, high and lifted up. About it stood the seraphims: each had six wings; with twain he did fly, with twain he covered his feet, with twain he covered his face.' To cover the face is a sign or fruit of bashfulness, as in Rebekah, Gen. 24:65. The face of an angel is void of all spots and wrinkles, it is full of beauty and brightness, a most excellent face. 'And all the council, looking steadfastly on him, beheld his face as if it had been the face of an angel,' Acts 6:15. Yet this face, as excellent as it is, they cover, as it were, ashamed of it before that God who alone is excellent.

iv. He is so incomparably excellent that he humbleth himself to take notice of his perfect spirits, his heavenly host, and their perfect service in heaven. It is not only great and infinite condescension with him to observe the highest persons on earth, as kings and princes, and the holiest persons on earth, as the most eminent saints, and the highest and holiest performances of these saints, but it is boundless humiliation in him to look upon, with the least respect, the perfect spirits of just men, the principalities and powers that are in heaven, and their pure, perfect worship and service: Ps. 113:5, 6, 'Who is like unto the Lord our God, who dwelleth on high, who humbleth himself to behold the things that are in heaven?'

v. He is so incomparably excellent that he is above the highest adoration and worship of his creatures. Worship is the most high, and honourable of all our works. Blessing and praising God is the most high and honourable act of worship; therefore this is that part of worship which suits the highest and honourablest state of the creature in heaven, and must continue forever. As all our graces, of faith, and hope, and patience, &c., shall ere long be melted into love, and joy, and delight, so all our duties, of confession, petition, hearing and reading the word, receiving the sacraments, shall all be melted into praise and thanksgiving: Rev. 7:11, 12, 'And the angels and elders that stood about the throne fell on their faces before the throne, and worshipped, saying, Amen, blessing, and honour, and thanksgiving, be unto our God, forever;' and therefore David calls upon angels and the heavenly host to praise God, Ps. 148:2, 3. But this incomparably excellent God is above all this worship, this highest worship, though he be not above it so as to despise it, Ps. 50:15, 23, yet he is above it, so as to exceed it; that his saints and angels, though their powers are enlarged to the uttermost, though the strings of their faculties are wound and screwed up to the highest pitch and peg to sound forth his praise, even then they will fall infinitely short of praising and blessing him according to his deserts: Neh. 9:5, 'Blessed be thy glorious name, which is exalted above all blessing and praise.' He doth not say the name of God is exalted above the blessing and praise of men, of saints on earth in their imperfect state, nor above the blessing and praise of spirits of just men in heaven made perfect, but above all blessing and praise, above the blessing and praise of men, of angels, of the holiest men, of the highest angels, above all blessing and praise whatsoever and of whomsoever.

vi. He is so incomparably excellent that his excellencies are beyond the understanding and apprehension of men and angels. The excellency of God is not only beyond all our expressions, verbal in our words, vital or real in our lives, but also beyond all our apprehensions. A fluent tongue may speak much of the excellency of God; an enlarged rational understanding can apprehend much more. The mind of man is much wider than his mouth; but the excellency of God is infinitely beyond all our apprehensions of him. His works are unsearchable, Rom. 11:33. 'Lo, he goeth by me, and I see him not; he passeth on, and I perceive him not,' Job 9:11. He goeth by me in his works, he passeth by me in the operations of his hands, and I perceive him not. There are such motions of God in the heavenly bodies, earthly plants, ordinary providences, the growth of a child in the womb, &c., that men are nonplussed at them, they are at a loss about the nature, reason, and mode or gradual progressions of them. How much more is his being unsearchable, and his essence past finding out? If his footsteps are inconceivable and invisible, much more is his face; if his works cannot be apprehended, much less can his nature; because his works are in some respects finite, as they are terminated on limited beings, and they are also many of them visible, and so obvious to our senses; but his essence is wholly and altogether, and in all respects infinite, and is no way visible or liable to apprehension by our senses: 1 Tim. 6:16, 'Who dwelleth in that light that is inaccessible.' As no mortal eye can behold the sun in its full strength, (the attempt of which, according to some, hath struck the adventurers blind,) so no creature whatsoever can apprehend the incomparable God in his full beauty and brightness, in his boundless excellency and perfection. It is the voice of God to Moses, 'Thou canst not see my face, for no man can see me and live,' Exod. 33:20. No man clothed with a mortal body, or in this estate of imperfection, can behold an extraordinary created appearance of God, but he is thereat filled with fears and frights, Job 4:12–15, and 21:22; Dan. 10:8, 16, 17; Hab. 3:16. No man, no, nor angel, can behold God in his infinite essence, to the utmost of his perfections, but would be thereat crumbled into nothing.

Reader, if God be thus incomparably excellent, that he is excellency itself, the standard of all excellency, that angels hide their heads as ashamed of themselves before him, that he condescendeth to shew the least respect to his high and perfect host in heaven, that he is infinitely above all their blessings and praises, all their conceptions and apprehensions, what praise, what honour, what glory shouldst thou give to this God! Though thou art unable to give him all the glory that is due to his name, yea, the thousand thousandth part thereof, yet do thou give him all the glory thy mind, will, heart, affections, all thy faculties united together, and enlarged to the utmost, can possibly give him. Say to thy soul, 'Bless the Lord, O my soul, and all within me praise his holy name,' Ps. 103:1.

XXVI

COMFORT TO THEM THAT HAVE THE INCOMPARABLE GOD FOR THEIR PORTION

III. Thirdly, This doctrine may be useful, by way of comfort, to all the people of God. If God be an incomparable God, then they are incomparably blessed who take him for their God, who have him for their happiness. Every person or people is happy or miserable, as the God is whom they serve, as that is in which they place their felicity; for nothing can give out more happiness to another than it hath in itself. That good must of necessity be first in the cause, either eminently or formally, which is conveyed from it to the effect. Those who serve the flesh, as their god and chief good, must needs be miserable, Phil. 3:18; Rom. 16:18; because the flesh is a base and vile, Ps. 49:20, a weak and impotent, Isa. 31:3, a fraudulent and deceitful, Jer. 17:9, a fading and transitory god, Ps. 73:25; 1 Cor. 6:2-3. So they who own, and prize, and love the world as their god and chief good—of such we read, the covetous man is called an idolater, and covetousness idolatry, Eph. 5:5—are miserable, because their god is vain and empty, Eccles. 1:2, 3, piercing and vexatious, 1 Tim. 6:9, 10, uncertain and unsatisfying, Eccles. 5:10; 1 Tim. 6:17, frail, and not lasting, 1 Cor. 7:29, 30; Prov. 23:5. Thus they who have idols for their gods are miserable, because their gods are poor, pitiful, blind, deaf, and impotent deities. They have eyes, and see not the wants of their worshippers; they have ears, and hear not the supplications of their suppliants; they have hands, and work not for the relief of their servants' necessities, or their deliverance out of their distresses; and thence the prophet infers the misery of their makers and adorers: 'All that make them are like unto them,' blind, and deaf, and impotent as they are, falsehood and a lie, and vanity, and nothing as they are, 1 Cor. 8:4; 1 Sam. 12:24, and so is every one that trusteth in them, Ps. 115:5-9. But the person who, through Christ, hath an interest in this great God, the almighty, allwise, allsufficient God, is happy: 'Happy is the people whose God is the

Lord,' Ps. 144:15; and incomparably happy, because that God who is his portion and happiness is an incomparable God. Therefore, as the Scripture mentions God to be incomparable in excellency, it also mentions his people to be incomparable in felicity, and infers their incomparableness from his incomparableness who is their God.

The Holy Ghost tells us, none is like God; he hath no equal in worth and perfection: 'Who is a god like unto thee?' Exod. 15:11; 'Among all the gods there is none like to thee,' Ps. 86:6. And the Holy Ghost tells us also that no people is like the people of God, and that because God is theirs: 'Happy art thou, O Israel, who is like unto thee?' why, whence comes their incomparable happiness? Truly, from the incomparable God; 'Saved by the Lord, who is the shield of thine help, and the sword of thine excellency.' Again, 'What nation is so great, which hath God so nigh unto them?' Deut. 4:7. Israel at this time, to flesh and sense, seemed a most unhappy people; they were in a barren and howling wilderness, without a house to hide their heads in, without food, but what a miracle sent them in; without raiment, but what was on their backs; without any dealings or converse with other people; nay, in the midst of cruel and potent enemies, they must fight their way to Canaan against walled towns and sturdy giants; and yet, even in this plight, they are the happiest people under the cope of heaven; because the God of heaven, the incomparable God, was nigh to them. David asserts God's incomparable majesty, and thence Israel's incomparable felicity: 2 Sam. 7:22, 23, 'Wherefore thou art great, O Lord, there is none like thee.' What followeth thence? 'And what nation at this day is like unto thy people, even like Israel?' Reader, if thou art once effectually called, if thou art a regenerated, sanctified person, know to thy comfort, and rejoice therein, that this incomparable God is thine. 2. That all his incomparable excellencies are thine. 3. That this incomparable God, with all his incomparable perfections, will be thine forever.

1. This incomparable God is thine. That God who hath no superior, no equal, no fellow, is thine. He that is, and there is none else, Isa. 46:9, is thine: he that is that he is, Exod. 3:14, is thine. Thou hast a propriety in him, and a title to him. This is the great privilege of heaven's favourites: 'Behold the tabernacle of God is with men, and he will dwell with them, and they shall be his people, and he will be their God,' Rev. 21:3. This is the great promise, the sum, the substance of all the promises: 'I will be their God, and they shall be my people,' Jer. 31:33. This is the great prayer of all that know how to pray, or what to pray for, Ps. 80:12, and 4:6; Exod. 33:15; Jer. 14:8. This is

the great purchase of the Son of God, 1 Pet. 3:18. His name is therefore Immanuel, God with us.

This is heaven, itself, the very heaven of heavens; for it is not the place, but his presence, which makes heaven to be heaven: 'In thy presence is fulness of joy, and at thy right hand are pleasures forevermore,' Ps. 16:11. Once more; this is the highest, the chiefest, the greatest gift which the infinite God can give to thee. When he giveth thee riches, and honours, and friends, and relations, he can give thee greater things; when he giveth thee sacraments, and Sabbaths, and seasons of grace, he can give thee greater things; when he giveth thee pardon of sin, peace of conscience, the graces of his Spirit, he giveth thee great things, but yet he can give thee greater; but when he giveth thee himself, he giveth thee the greatest gift that himself, though infinite in bounty, can give. Oh how sweet is that term of propriety, my God, my God. The Redeemer himself rolled it in his mouth over and over, as if he could never suck out the sweetness in it: 'Him that overcometh will I make a pillar in the house of my God; and I will write on him the name of my God, and the name of the city of my God, which is the new Jerusalem, which cometh down from my God,' Rev. 3:12. David dwells on it as one unwilling to leave it, Ps. 18:1, 2.

Reader, oh what cause hast thou to triumph in thy happiness, that the infinite God is thine! 'Fear not, I am thine,' Isa. 41. Sceptres, and kingdoms, and honours, and possessions, and friends, and relations, and liberty, and peace, and health, and strength, are not thine possibly, but God is thine; he that is all these, and more than these, is thine; he is thine own God—even (mark) 'our own God shall bless us,' Ps. 67:6. Thou canst not call anything outward thine own. Thy estate is not thine own: 'I will take away my corn, and my wine, and my oil,' Hos. 2:9, Hag. 2:8. Thy relations are not thine own: Ezek. 16:20, 21, 'My children which thou hast born to me.' Thy credit is not thine own; no, thy very graces are not thine own, Cant. 4:16. Nay, thou thyself art not thy own: 1 Cor. 6:20, 'Ye are not your own.' Thy body is not thine own, 1 Cor. 6:16; nor your souls: Ezek. 18:3, 4, 'All souls are mine.' But God is thy own God, thy own glory, thy own exceeding joy, Ps. 93:4.

2. All the incomparable excellencies of this God, his incomparable word and works, are thine. As all he is, is thine, so all he hath is thine, all he can be is thine, all he hath done is thine, all he can do is thine: 1 Cor. 3:22, 'All is thine.' All his incomparable attributes are thine. His incomparable power

is thine to protect thee, Gen. 15:1, 2; Exod. 15:9–12; his incomparable wisdom is thine to direct thee, Ps. 73:23; his incomparable mercy is thine to pity and relieve thee in thy miseries, Judges 10:16; his incomparable grace is thine to pardon all thine iniquities, Micah 7:18; Exod. 34:6, 7; his incomparable love is thine to refresh and delight thy soul, Ps. 21:5, 6; his incomparable justice is thine to accept thee as righteous for the sake of his Son, Rom. 3:24; his incomparable faithfulness is thine to fulfil all the gracious promises which he hath made to thee, Ps. 89:33, 34; his incomparable majesty and beauty and glory are thine, to make thee great, and render thee comely and glorious forever, Ezek. 16:14; Isa. 43:4; his incomparable joys and pleasures are thine to feed on, and be filled with, Ps. 36:8; Mat. 25:21; his incomparable works are thine; his works of creation, Ps. 37:11, Mat. 5:4; his works of providence, Rom. 8:28; for your sakes I have sent to Babylon, Isa. 43:14, and 43:4; his work of redemption is yours, John 10:15; Gal. 2:20; Rev. 1:5, 6; his incomparable word is thine, indited for thee, sanctified to thee, making thee wise to salvation. It is therefore called their word, the word of their testimony, Rev. 12:11. 'Whatsoever things were written were written for our instruction, that we through patience and comfort of the Scriptures might have hope,' Rom. 15:4.

3. This incomparable God, and all his incomparable excellencies, will be thine forever. His incomparable eternity will be thine, and so long as he is God he will be thy God. When the sensualist's god is gone, thy God will remain; when the worldling's god fails him, thy God will not forsake thee; when all thine honours, riches, friends, relations, leave thee, thy God will abide with thee: 'This God is our God forever and ever,' Ps. 48:14. Not for a day, or week, or month, or year, or age, but forever and ever; not for a thousand years, or a thousand generations, or millions of millions of generations, but forever and ever; not for as many millions of ages as there are stars in heaven, drops in the sea, creatures great and small in both worlds, but forever. Oh happy conjunction of propriety with eternity, this God is our God forever and ever! Thine immortal soul hath an immortal God, an immortal good: 'Thou shalt ever be with this incomparable Lord.' Comfort thy soul in the midst of all the persecutions and afflictions that befall thee in this world, with these words: 1 Thes. 4:16–18, 'For the Lord himself shall descend from heaven with a shout, with the voice of the archangel, and with the trump of God: and the dead in Christ shall rise first. Then we which are alive and remain, shall be caught up together with him in the clouds, to meet the Lord in the air: and so shall we ever be with the Lord. Wherefore comfort one another with these words.'